RENEWALS 458-45/4.
DATE DUE

ILL# 15702483

ILL# 21899467

ILL# 31994430

GAYLORD   PRINTED IN U.S.A.

Metadata

for information management
and retrieval

Metadata

for information management
and retrieval

David Haynes

facet publishing

Published by
Facet Publishing
7 Ridgmount Street
London WC1E 7AE

Facet Publishing (formerly Library Association Publishing) is wholly owned by CILIP: the Chartered Institute of Library and Information Professionals.

First published 2004

British Library Cataloguing in Publication Data
A catalogue record for this book is available from the British Library.

ISBN 1-85604-489-0

Typeset in 11/14 pt Basel and URW Grotesk by Facet Publishing.
Printed and made in Great Britain by MPG Books Ltd, Bodmin, Cornwall.

Contents

Acknowledgements

Preparation of this book would not have been possible without the considerable support and assistance of many individuals. Although it is not possible to mention everyone I hope that they will recognize their contributions in this book and will accept this acknowledgement as thanks.

I am particularly grateful to Janet Liebster, the MD of CILIP Enterprises and colleagues at CILIP for their active interest and encouragement. I would also like to thank staff in Information Services at CILIP for their help with references. The editorial and production staff at Facet Publishing have helped to ensure the consistency and quality of the final product. Adjoa Boateng and Louise Stone of CILIP Consultancy Services both helped with research and reference checking

Many colleagues in the wider profession helped to clarify specific points about the use of metadata. I would especially like to thank Michael Day of UKOLN for his detailed and comprehensive comments on the original manuscript. Thanks are also due to Stuart Ede, Brian Green, John Douglas and Elspeth Hyams for allowing time for discussion of issues raised by my research.

Many institutions and organizations have contributed by allowing me to reproduce text or diagrams in the book, including the Health and Safety Executive (use of extracts from their thesaurus and business classification scheme); the British Library, the M25 Consortium of Academic Libraries and Westminster Public Libraries (with Geac) (use of screen shots from their library catalogues); and the Department of Health (reproduction of a page with metadata from their website).

Microsoft Explorer™ has been used in the majority of instances to capture screenshots from the internet and Microsoft PowerPoint™ has been used to develop many of the diagrams and figures.

I would like to thank William Blacklock for his support throughout the project.

Preface

Why this book?

One of the key challenges facing information managers today is the need to inter-relate different sources and types of information, whether it be in an internet search across a range of resources with different formats, data structures and description standards or an e-commerce system that needs to exchange data between proprietary applications in order to complete a transaction. Understanding the structure and architecture of the data allows this to occur and metadata is the means by which this happens. Using metadata to record data about information sources allows an initial assessment of compatibility and provides an avenue for merging information or for exchanging information between systems. In other words the concept of 'interoperability' has become a major theme for information managers and ultimately for users. Using metadata to manage information resources is now an established part of the work of diverse groups of professionals, from web managers and librarians to IT managers and systems designers.

Those responsible for specifying, designing and setting up systems, need to know about metadata, as do those information professionals who operate retrieval systems. They need to manage metadata. Information professionals are being asked to take on the responsibility for ensuring consistency of information so that it is accessible and can be retrieved easily by those who need it. This book describes some of the options available for managing metadata and illustrates this with examples from the library, information and records management domains.

Until the publication of Caplan (2003) there were no general texts that brought together current developments in metadata applications from the perspective of library and information professionals. There are several recent texts on specific aspects of metadata, often from the perspective of IT managers and programmers (Tannenbaum, 2002; Tozer, 1999), but very few providing a general introduction.

In the late 1990s, when the library and information profession began to turn its attention to metadata, articles started to appear in the professional press outlining what metadata was and debating whether there was a difference between creating metadata and cataloguing information resources. This book takes the view that library catalogues are metadata collections and that many of the principles of cataloguing apply more generally to metadata. For instance cataloguing rules ensure consistency, and adherence to standards for data encoding and the use of authority lists helps to eliminate ambiguities. The skills of librarians and information scientists are therefore directly relevant to metadata development, implementation and management. Some early titles recognize this and are directed specifically at library and information science professionals (Hudgins, Agnew and Brown, 1999; Baca, 1998). The intention of this book is to carry on from where they left off by describing recent progress in metadata standards and applications and focusing on the concepts behind metadata. It looks at the way in which metadata is applied to different purposes. It is intended to be complementary to Caplan (2003) who provides a description of metadata standards for different domains. This book takes a complementary approach by dealing with metadata thematically and illustrating the principles of metadata with examples.

Many of the metadata standards emerging during the late 1990s have stabilized and are being adopted currently in libraries, museums, archives, government websites and corporate intranets. Some software suppliers are building metadata fields into the records structure and in some areas they depend on it for the management of information in data repositories (e.g. databases, library catalogues and rights management systems). The Dublin Core guidelines and other metadata schemes are now widely used for corporate intranets, local government and electronic records management systems. Where there are specific, specialist requirements, information managers are starting to develop extensions to existing schemes as application profiles. Metadata is used to enable interoperation between systems and this is an essential part of information systems today. Metadata standards are stabilizing and it is now a good time to capture this diverse experience and emerging practice in a book that is designed to be accessible to a wide audience.

If metadata is to be adopted successfully, it is vital to have a corpus of information workers who are capable of applying it, managers who understand its significance and specialists capable of extending existing metadata standards to new application areas. The library and information profession in particular is a group with many of the skills already in place to manage metadata schemes and to apply metadata to digital objects such as electronic documents, digitized images, sound recordings and data repositories. However, there first needs to be an understanding of the vocabulary of metadata. Information workers need to be able to see how their skills can be applied in the context of metadata use. Now is the time to prepare a generation of information workers to operate effectively in an environment that makes extensive use of metadata.

The book touches on many related issues that are covered elsewhere. For instance work on XML, an increasingly important language for describing web resources and for expressing metadata, is covered in Goldfarb and Prescod (2001). Information architecture is covered by a number of excellent texts and volumes of essays such as Gilchrist and Mahon (2004). For an overview of current developments in metadata I recommend the *International Yearbook of Library and Information Management 2003–2004* (Gorman, 2004).

Audience

This book is aimed at two principal audiences: the information professionals who want to develop their knowledge and skills in order to manage metadata effectively, and managers who are faced with strategic decisions about adoption of IT applications that use metadata.

For both groups this book provides a general overview of metadata and an understanding of the issues that affect users of information systems. It can also be used as an introductory text for IT managers prior to reading more technical IT titles such as Tannenbaum (2002) and Tozer (1999).

The intention of this book is to help specialists and professionals who manage information resources to become easily conversant with this important and rapidly developing area. It is addressed to all those who need to know about metadata and what it can do, including:

- library and information professionals who want to educate themselves about a core area of skills as part of their continuing professional development
- graduate students (masters and postgraduate diploma students) in librarianship, information science and records management
- knowledge managers and information architects who design and set up information systems
- archivists and records managers who plan to implement strategies to enhance the retrieval performance of electronic document and records management systems

- IT managers who need to gain an appreciation of retrieval issues in the context of information management strategies
- informed users and intelligent clients who may be responsible for corporate strategic issues and wish to appreciate the range of possibilities offered by metadata.

Organization of the book

This book is divided into ten chapters and the intention is that readers can consult specific chapters of particular interest, or read the entire book as a narrative work.

Chapter 1 – Introduction considers how metadata arose and why it is important in the electronic environment, and discusses some common definitions of metadata. The chapter introduces the five purposes of metadata which provide the structure for the main part of the book.

Chapter 2 – Describing and expressing metadata gives a more detailed definition of metadata and describes the main concepts associated with it such as mark-up languages, data elements and metadata schemas. It also touches on the modelling concepts used for database design and development. It is illustrated with examples of metadata in different application environments.

Chapter 3 – Standards and data models looks at current development in metadata standards for the internet (such as Dublin Core), government websites and work in other sectors to develop data models such as the Functional Requirements for Bibliographic Records (FRBR) model for cataloguing resources.

The next five chapters are organized around the five purposes of metadata defined in the first chapter.

Chapter 4 – Purpose i: Resource description reviews ways in which information resources are described using metadata from websites through to bibliographic citations.

Chapter 5 – Purpose ii: Information retrieval reviews ways in which subject indexing, controlled vocabularies, classifications and other ways of describing content are handled as metadata. It also considers retrieval on the internet and retrieval of different types of resource including text, multimedia and graphics images, and explores some of the techniques that have evolved to deal with these types of material.

Chapter 6 – Purpose iii: Management of information introduces the concept of metadata as a tool for managing information. It describes document and records management, content management systems and intranet applications. The chapter also covers education and e-learning as well as the specific issue of digital preservation.

Chapter 7 – Purpose iv: Rights management, ownership and authenticity deals with information security, authority control, version control, authenticity of information and legal admissibility of electronic evidence. It describes some of the systems that have arisen in the book trade and the music industry to deal with ownership of copyright and payment of royalties.

Chapter 8 – Purpose v: Interoperability and e-commerce considers the role of metadata in the interoperability between systems and how this is facilitated by the use of metadata standards. The role of metadata as an enabler for e-commerce is also considered.

The last two chapters provide a more general treatment of metadata and some speculations about the future.

Chapter 9 – Managing metadata considers some of the techniques used to make metadata interoperable, including crosswalks and registries. The chapter describes metadata in terms of an information lifecycle and considers the role of administrative metadata.

Chapter 10 – Looking forward – the future considers the impact that metadata is likely to have on the wider area of information management and the possibilities for the development of a new discipline.

David Haynes

References and further sources of information

Baca, M. (ed.) (1998) Introduction to Metadata: pathways to digital information, Los Angeles, CA, Getty Information Institute.

Caplan, P. (2003) *Metadata for all Librarians*, Chicago, IL, American Library Association.

Gilchrist, A. and Mahon, B. (eds) (2004) *Information Architecture: designing information environments for purpose*, London, Facet Publishing.

Goldfarb C. F. and Prescod P. (2001) *The XML Handbook*, 3rd edn, Upper Saddle River, NJ, Prentice Hall.

Gorman G. E. (ed.) (2004) *Metadata Applications and Management: International Yearbook of Library and Information Management 2003–2004*, London, Facet Publishing.

Hudgins J., Agnew G. and Brown E. (1999) *Getting Mileage out of Metadata: applications for the library*, LITA Guides No. 5, Chicago, IL, American Library Association.

Tannenbaum, A. (2002) *Metadata Solutions: using metamodels, repositories, XML and enterprise portals to generate information on demand*, Boston, MA, Addison-Wesley.

Tozer, G. (1999) *Metadata Management for Information Control and Business Success*, Boston, MA, Artech House.

Chapter 1
Introduction

overview

THIS CHAPTER INTRODUCES **the idea of metadata and illustrates it with some early examples of the use of metadata concepts before the term 'metadata' was coined. The development of metadata is placed in the context of the history of cataloguing as well as parallel developments in other disciplines. This leads to discussion of the definitions of 'metadata' and a suggested form of words that is appropriate for this book. Some examples of metadata from library catalogues and websites are used to illustrate the concept. The chapter then considers why metadata is important in the information culture that many people work in. This provides a way of assessing the models of metadata in terms of its uses. The chapter concludes with a five-point model for the use (or purposes) of metadata.**

Metadata is important in the information society. It is having a profound impact on most aspects of information work and is an enabler of the information systems that underpin the knowledge economy, e-commerce and e-government. Understanding what metadata is and how it works is crucial for those working in the knowledge, information, cultural and learning sectors. Use of information modelling techniques associated with metadata analysis will help the next generation of information services providers and systems designers to deliver more effective services and systems. General users need to understand how metadata works in order to make best use of resources that are available on the internet, for instance, and to have an idea of where things might be going in future.

The historical background is the starting point for an understanding of metadata, what it is, and how it is used.

Some historical background

Library catalogues

Although the term 'metadata' is a recent one, many of the concepts and techniques of metadata creation, management and use originated with the development of library catalogues. Books (and scrolls) are repositories of information and a catalogue contains data about that information and can therefore be regarded as metadata. An understanding of what people tried to do before the term 'metadata' was coined helps to explain the concept of metadata. The historical background also gives a perspective on why metadata has become so important in recent years.

The idea of cataloguing information has been around at least since the Alexandria Library in ancient Egypt. Callimachus of Cyrene (305–235BC), the poet and author, was a librarian at Alexandria. He is widely credited with creating the first catalogue, the 'Pinakes', of the Alexandria Library's 500,000 scrolls. The catalogue was itself a work of 120 scrolls with titles grouped by subject and genre (Ellens, 1997). This was in effect the first recorded compilation of metadata.

In Western Europe library cataloguing developed in the ecclesiastical and, later, academic libraries. In the eighth century the books donated by Gregory the Great to the Church of St Clement in Rome were catalogued in the form of a prayer. During the same era, Alcuin of York (735–804) developed a metrical catalogue for the library at York Cathedral. Cataloguing developed so that by the 14th century the location of books started to appear in catalogue records and by the 16th century the first alphabetical arrangements began to appear. Up until that time catalogues were used as inventories of stock rather than for finding books or for managing collections.

Modern library catalogues date back to the French code of 1791, the first national cataloguing code with author entry which used catalogue cards and rules of accessioning and guiding. Cataloguing rules (an important aspect of metadata) were developed by Sir Anthony Panizzi for the British Museum Library and these were published in 1841. In the USA Charles A. Cutter prepared *Rules of a Dictionary Catalog*, which was published in 1876. The American Library Association and the Library Association in the UK both developed cataloguing rules around the turn of the century. This led to an agreement in 1904 to co-operate to produce an international cataloguing code which was published in separate American and British editions in 1908.

Later, the International Conference on Cataloguing Principles in Paris in 1961 established a set of principles on the choice and form of headings in author/title catalogues. These were incorporated into the first edition of the *Anglo-American Cataloguing Rules* (AACR) in 1967, published in two versions by the Library Association and the American Library Association. The Canadian Library Association, the British Library and the Library of Congress were closely involved in the Joint Steering Committee for the Revision of the AACR (Joint Steering Committee for Revision of AACR, 2002a).

The International Standard Bibliographic Descriptions (ISBDs) were developed by IFLA and have been incorporated into the second edition of the *Anglo-American Cataloguing Rules* (AACR2), published in 1988 and revised in 2002; they have been adopted by the Library of Congress, the National Library of Canada, the British Library and the Australian National Library (Joint Steering Committee for the Revision of AACR, 2002b). AACR2 specifies the sources of information used to describe a publication, the order in which the data elements appear and the punctuation used to separate the elements. This was an important development because it made catalogues more interchangeable and allowed for conversion into machine-readable form (Bowman, 2003).

Electronic catalogues

In the mid-1960s computers started being used for the purpose of cataloguing and a new standard for the data format of catalogue records, MARC (MAchine Readable Cataloguing), was established. MARC covers all kinds of library materials and is usable in automated library management systems. Although MARC was initially used to process and generate catalogue cards more quickly, libraries soon started to use it as a means of exchanging cataloguing data, which helped to reduce the cost of cataloguing original materials. The availability of MARC records stimulated the development of searchable electronic catalogues. The user benefited from wider access to searchable catalogues, and later on to union catalogues, which allowed them to search several library catalogues at once. Different versions of MARC emerged, largely based on national variations, for example USMARC, UKMARC and NORMARC. Although the different MARC versions were designed to reflect the particular needs and interests of different countries or communities of interest, they inhibited international exchange of records. It is only with the recent widespread adoption of MARC21 by the national bibliographic authorities that a degree of harmonization of national bibliographies is being achieved.

The growth of electronic catalogues and the development of textual databases able to handle summaries of published articles demanded new skills, which in turn contributed to the development of information science as a discipline. Information scientists developed many of the early electronic catalogues and bibliographic databases (Feather and Sturges, 1997). They adapted library cataloguing rules for an electronic environment and did much of the pioneering work on information retrieval theory, including the measures of precision and recall which are discussed in Chapter 5.

Although metadata was first used in library catalogues it is now widely used in records management, the publishing industry, the recording industry, government, the geospatial community and among statisticians. Metadata is widely used because it provides the tools to describe electronic information resources, allowing for more consistent retrieval, better management of data sources and exchange of data records between applications and organizations.

Origin of the term

Vellucci (1998) suggests that the term 'metadata' dates back to the 1960s but became established in the context of Database Management Systems (DBMSs) in the 1970s. Woodley (1999) traces the first reference to 'meta-data' back to a PhD dissertation on 'An infological approach to data bases' which made the distinction between:

- objects (real-world phenomena);
- information about the object; and
- data representing information about the object (i.e. metadata).

The term had begun to be widely used in the database research community by the mid-1970s in Northern Europe.

A parallel development occurred in the geographical information systems (GIS) community and in particular the digital spatial information discipline. In the late 1980s and early 1990s there was considerable activity within the GIS community to develop metadata standards to encourage interoperability between systems. Because government (especially local government) activity often requires data to describe location, there are significant benefits to be gained from a standard to describe location or spatial position across databases and agencies. The metadata associated with location data has allowed organizations to maintain their often considerable internal investments in geospatial data, while still co-operating with other organizations and institutions. Metadata is a way of sharing details of their data in catalogues of geographic information, clearing houses or via vendors of information. Metadata also gives users the information they need to process and interpret a particular set of geospatial data.

Metadata initiatives

In the mid-1990s the idea of a core set of semantics for web-based resources was put forward for categorizing the web and to enhance retrieval. This became known as the Dublin Core Metadata Initiative (DCMI), which has established a standard for describing web content and which is not discipline- or language-specific. The DCMI defines a set of data elements which can be used as containers for metadata. The metadata is embedded in the resources so that it is accessible to users and systems that use the web resource. DCMI is an ongoing initiative which continues to develop and elaborate the metadata standards for web applications (see Chapter 3, page 51 for more details).

This position is questioned by Gorman (2003) who suggests that metadata schemes such as Dublin Core are merely subsets of much more sophisticated frameworks such as MARC. He suggests that without authority control and use of controlled vocabularies, Dublin Core and other metadata schemes cannot achieve their aim of improving the precision and recall from a large database (such as web resources on the internet). His solution is that existing metadata standards should be enriched to bring them up to the standards of cataloguing. However, his arguments depend on a distinction being drawn between 'full cataloguing' and 'metadata'. An alternative view (and one supported in this book) is that catalogues are a form of metadata.

All of these approaches to metadata have begun to come together as the different communities have become aware of the others' activities and have started to work together. The DCMI involved the database and LIS communities from the beginning with the first workshop in 1995 in Dublin, Ohio, and has gradually drawn in other groups that manage and use metadata. Work has also gone into the development of crosswalks of standards so that it is possible to map the data elements of one metadata standard on to those of another. Bodies such as the International Organization for Standardization (ISO) are currently developing metadata standards and this activity is described in detail in Chapter 3.

Looking at existing trends, therefore, metadata is becoming more widely recognized and it is being included in the specification of IT applications and software products. For example, the UK government's specification for electronic document and records management systems specifies minimum metadata standards. In addition, content management systems are increasingly being called on to handle resources that contain embedded metadata so that the resulting web and intranet pages are retrievable and can be exchanged between different systems. As a result, manufacturers of digital hardware and suppliers of software applications are incorporating metadata standards into their products and this in turn will stimulate further uptake of metadata.

This brief history of metadata demonstrates that it had several starting points and arose independently in different quarters. In the 1990s, there was growing awareness about metadata, and the work of bodies such as the Dublin Core Metadata Initiative has done a great deal to raise the profile of metadata and its widespread use in different communities. It has become an established part of the information environment today. However, its history does mean that there are distinct differences in the understanding of metadata and it is necessary to develop some universal definitions of the term.

What is metadata?

At this stage it is worth interrogating the concept of metadata more fully. The previous section described how the concept of metadata arose from several different intellectual traditions. This is reflected in the different uses of metadata that are described later in this chapter (pp 12–17). They depend on the priorities of the communities that are using it. This leads to speculation on whether there is a common understanding of what metadata is, and whether there is a definition that is generally applicable.

Metadata was originally referred to as 'meta-data', with an emphasis on the two-word fragments that make up the term. The word fragment 'meta', which comes from the Greek μετα, translates into several distinct meanings in English. In this context it can be taken to mean a higher or ulterior view of the word it prefixes. In other words metadata is data about data, or data that describes data or information.

Many of the available definitions focus on the function that metadata performs. For instance Tozer looks at metadata from the perspective of database management systems. So in this definition metadata is for control of data and it is seen as contributing to business success:

> A more useful perspective is gained by seeing metadata as the means by which the structure and behavior of data is recorded, controlled, and published across an organization. (Tozer, 1999, xix)

Some in the library and information community have taken a similar approach, also defining metadata in terms of function or purpose. However in this context metadata has more wide-ranging purposes and includes purposes such as retrieval and management of information resources. It also includes rights management and information about the provenance of data. Aspects of access control relate to the information retrieval purpose of metadata:

> any data that aids in the identification, description and location of networked electronic resources. . . . Another important function provided by metadata is control of the electronic resource, whether through ownership and provenance metadata for validating information and tracking use; rights and permissions metadata for controlling access; or content ratings metadata, a key component of some Web filtering applications.
> (Hudgins, Agnew and Brown, 1999)

Gilliland-Swetland takes a similarly wide-ranging view of the purpose of metadata in her definition. Metadata is described in terms of the range of uses to which it is put. Interestingly she specifically mentions paper documents as being within the scope of metadata. This is a position that is endorsed in this book in contrast to an earlier definition of metadata which focused on digital objects. The Gilliland-Swetland definition of metadata is:

> there is more to metadata than description; a more inclusive conceptualisation of metadata is needed as information professionals consider the range of their activities that may end up being incorporated into digital information systems. Repositories also create metadata relating to the administration, accessioning, preservation, and use of collections. Acquisition records, exhibition catalogs, and use data are all examples of these, even though they are largely still created in paper form. (Gilliland-Swetland, 1998, 1)

For many people, metadata is seen almost exclusively in the context of the internet and access to web resources. This is evident in the definition devised by the UK government's Office of the e-Envoy (OeE), which is particularly relevant for web resources, again describing it in terms of its uses. It emphasizes resource discovery and also mentions management, without elaborating on it:

> Metadata can be understood as data about data, a tool enabling users, seekers and owners of information resources to find and manage them.
>
> (UK Office of the e-Envoy, 2003)

These detailed definitions or explanations of metadata are based on specific application areas such as libraries or web resources and are too specific to apply across the range of applications that will be considered in this book. Some of them imply a definition by describing the way in which metadata is applied. Although the meaning of metadata depends on the context and the community that is using it, there is some benefit in adopting a general definition that can apply across the full range of contexts that it may be found in.

Although there is an attractive simplicity in the original definition: 'Metadata is data about data', it is not adequate to describe the complexity of the subject and the range of situations in which it might be used.

A further description is proposed to cover the range of situations in which it might be applied, while still making meaningful distinctions from the wider set of data about objects. If the object (say a packet of cereal on the supermarket shelf) is not an information resource, then data about that object is merely data, not metadata. Our definition of metadata is therefore as follows:

> Metadata is data that describes the content, format or attributes of a data record or information resource. It can be used to describe highly structured resources or unstructured information such as text documents. Metadata can be applied to description of: electronic resources; digital data (including digital images); and to printed documents such as books, journals and reports. Metadata can be embedded within the information resource (as is often the case with web resources) or it can be held separately in a database.

What does metadata look like?

Having considered some definitions of metadata, it is useful to see some examples. What does it look like? Some metadata is never seen by humans, because it is transient and used for exchange of data between

Figure 1.1

```
100    1     $aPedley, Paul
245    10    $aEssential law for information professionals/ $cPaul
Pedley
260          $aLondon: $bFacet, $c2003
300          $axviii, 222p.; $c24cm
```

Example of a MARC21 catalogue record

systems. Visible examples of metadata range from HTML metatags on web pages to MARC records used for exchanging cataloguing data between library management systems. It can be expressed in a structured language such as XML (Extensible Mark-up Language) and may follow guidelines or schema for particular domains of activity.

The two examples here show metadata associated with different objects. Figure 1.1 is an extract taken from a library catalogue and describes a book in a library, using the MARC21 standard ISO 2709:1996. It uses a three-digit tag for labelling fields, so that '100' represents the author field, '245' represents the title field, '260' the publication details and '300' the format of the publication. Immediately after the field tag is a two-digit modifier, generally used to give extra information to the computer, such as how the content of the field is to be sorted. Within each field are subfields separated by '$' delimiters. In field 100, subfield $a is the author name. This use of field tags, modifiers and delimiters ensures that different systems are able to interpret the data in a consistent way and know how to treat all information of a particular sort. It also ensures consistent layout of standard documents such as catalogue cards or screen displays. MARC is an early example of metadata used to allow interoperability.

The second example, Figure 1.2, is of metadata embedded in an HTML web page. The 'DC' label refers to the Dublin Core Element Set, a metadata standard for describing web-based resources. This extract is from an official government web page, and demonstrates how the content of the web page can be enriched with metadata.

Figure 1.2

```
<meta name="DC.Identifier" scheme="URI"
content="http://www.doh.gov.uk/nsf/diabetes"/>
<meta name="DC.Creator" lang="en" content="Department of Health, UK"
/>
<meta name="DC.Title" lang="en" content="NHS National Service
Framework for Diabetes: standards"/>
<meta name="DC.Subject" lang="en"
content="doh.gov.uk/nsf/diabetes; diabetes; department of health; NHS,
England; united kingdom; public health; uk; national health service;
NSF; National Service Framework;"/>
<meta name="DC.Description" lang="en"
content="Full text of National Service Framework for Diabetes:
standards - including additional material, service models and
intervention details"/>
<meta name="DC.Date.created" scheme="ISO8601" content="2000-08-27"/>
```

Extract from the source coding of a web page, www.doh.gov.uk/nsf/diabetes/delivery/foreward.htm
© Crown copyright

The extract shows metadata arranged into different elements corresponding to fields. The name of the metadata standard is embedded in the coding – in this case Dublin Core (see pp 51–4). For instance in the line:

```
<meta name="DC.Creator" lang="en" content="Department of Health, UK"/>
```

the content of the Dublin Core metadata element 'Creator' is expressed in English and the content of that data element (i.e. the creator) is the Department of Health, UK. This kind of element can be generated automatically. The actual web page from which this is extracted is shown in Figure 1.3.

Figure 1.3

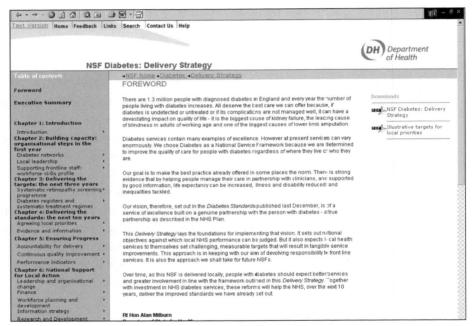

Web page containing metadata (UK Department of Health, 2003)
© Crown copyright

Why is metadata important?

A more comprehensive understanding of metadata can be developed from studying the above examples. The development of cataloguing over two millennia has provided a set of tools for describing published information. This has been drawn on by the web community. Correspondingly the growth of the internet has focused public attention on the importance of information retrieval and management and has stimulated the development of tools to improve retrieval performance. Having a clear understanding of what metadata is and how it works also provides a means of managing of information resources more effectively. In answering the question 'Why is metadata important?' several arguments emerge:

- *Metadata enhances retrieval performance* – Metadata can improve retrieval by establishing a context for individual descriptors. For instance the word 'Green' in the Creator or Author field indicates the name of an individual, whereas 'green' in the title of a document may be a subject retrieval term. Appropriate metadata tags around the different data elements allow search engines to seek information in a more discriminating way. The presence of a subject field (metadata element) can be used as a prompt for entering keywords, or for use of controlled indexing terms to describe the document. Knowing how metadata works provides information managers with a mechanism for indexing documents more precisely.
- *Metadata provides a way of managing electronic digital objects* – Many software packages use metadata as a way of managing electronic resources, whether it is for records retention schedules or for digital preservation. Content management systems, for instance, use metadata to track when a digital object was last updated or verified, who was responsible for its creation and whether any special access conditions apply. Unlike paper records or printed publications there is not a long tradition of managing digital objects and metadata provides a focus for the establishment of standard practices. It is the metadata associated with digital objects that provides a common format for management and manipulation of resources.
- *Metadata can help to determine the authenticity of data* – Metadata provides an audit trail to establish ownership and authenticity of a digital object such as an electronic document or image. The history of what has happened to a document or record in its life becomes an important part of this. Metadata provides evidence about the provenance of a resource and this underpins good governance, transparency and accountability. This is increasingly important for the many organizations that depend on electronic records rather than paper files. It becomes necessary to demonstrate that the electronic document has been kept securely, it is a complete record, and it has not been tampered with. Metadata provides evidence for the integrity of an electronic document.

This is particularly important in a legal context where electronic documents or physical records may be used, for example as evidence in legal proceedings.

- *Metadata is the key to interoperability* – Interoperability depends on the exchange of metadata between systems to establish the nature of the data being transferred and how it should be handled. E-commerce is one example of interoperating, where several different proprietary systems may need to exchange data. Access to metadata helps to establish the protocols of exchange of data and ways in which it might be exploited. Another example is in the development of e-government initiatives around the world, where there is a move towards common standards for data held by the different government departments or ministries, to allow greater exchange of data and delivery of 'joined-up' government services. Metadata fulfils an important role in enabling this to work, by establishing standards for data elements and by providing information about the data on one system so that it can be processed and used by other systems or departments.

- *Metadata is the future* – An increasing number of software and systems suppliers are working to metadata standards or are creating their own proprietary standards for metadata. The growth of e-commerce depends on metadata for exchange of data between applications. Many industries are developing their own e-commerce infrastructure to allow software from different suppliers to work together and exchange data. As we saw above, the e-government initiatives around the world are underpinned by the concept of interoperability and this in turn often depends on metadata standards. For instance the UK government has developed its own metadata standard, the e-Government Metadata Standard (eGMS) for use on government websites, based on the Dublin Core Metadata Element Set (DCMES). Metadata generated by content management systems is seeing a renaissance on the internet after its initial use for subject description. Metadata standards are being used by portal software and to provide access to the information content of websites.

These five arguments for the importance of metadata provide a way of assessing the purposes to which metadata is put.

The purposes of metadata

The recent emphasis on building consensus between different communities of interest has led to collaborative efforts to develop international standards for metadata. One of the main drivers for the evolution of metadata standards within each community is the use to which the metadata is put – its purpose. Even within the library and information profession, a range of metadata purposes have been identified. Two of the most useful models have been adopted as a basis for the general model of metadata used throughout this book.

In the first model Day (2001) suggests that metadata has seven distinct purposes. He starts with resource description – identifying and describing the entity that the metadata is about. The second purpose is focused on information retrieval, which in the context of web resources is called 'resource discovery'. This is one of the primary focuses of the Dublin Core metadata initiative. He recognizes that metadata is used for administering and managing resources (Purpose 3) – for instance flagging items for update after set periods of time have elapsed. The fourth purpose, intellectual property rights, is very important in the context of e-commerce, although e-commerce has not been listed as a purpose in its own right. Again this is possibly a reflection of the fact that the model is oriented towards web resources. Documenting software and hardware environments, the fifth purpose, provides contextual information about a resource, but will not apply to every resource. This could be seen as one aspect of resource description. His sixth purpose, preservation management, is a specialized form of administrative metadata and could be incorporated into Purpose 3. Finally providing information on context and authenticity is very important in a number of areas, particularly records management, where being able to demonstrate the authenticity of a record is a part of good governance, and for collection management where the provenance of individual items may affect their value. The seven purposes of metadata identified by Day can be summarized as follows:

1 Resource description
2 Resource discovery
3 Administration and management of resources
4 Record of intellectual property rights
5 Documenting software and hardware environments
6 Preservation management of digital resources
7 Providing information on context and authenticity.

Gilliland-Swetland (1998) and later Caplan (2003) take a slightly different approach, classifying metadata into categories according to its purpose. The use of metadata is categorized into more specific sub-categories. This means that a metadata scheme as well as individual metadata elements could fall into several different categories simultaneously. Gilliland-Swetland provides some useful examples of the metadata that falls under each of type (see Table 1.1). There is some common ground with Day, in that they both identify administration (equivalent to management and administration), description (encompassing information retrieval or resource discovery) and preservation as key purposes or types of metadata. The technical metadata in Gilliland-Swetland corresponds to 'Documenting hardware and software environments' in Day. The 'Use' metadata could include transactional data as would be seen in an e-commerce system or could provide an audit trail for documents in a records management system.

Table 1.1 Different types of metadata and their functions, extracted from Gilliland-Swetland

Type	Definition	Examples
Administrative	Metadata used in managing and administering information resources	• Acquisition information • Rights and reproduction tracking • Documentation of legal access requirements • Location information • Selection criteria for digitization • Version control
Descriptive	Metadata used to describe or identify information resources	• Cataloguing records • Finding aids • Specialized indexes • Hyperlinked relationships between resources • Annotations by users
Preservation	Metadata related to the information resources	• Documentation of physical condition of preservation management of resources • Documentation of actions taken to preserve physical and digital versions of resources, e.g. data refreshing and migration
Technical	Metadata related to how a system functions or metadata behaves	• Hardware and software documentation • Digitization information, e.g. formats, compression ratios, scaling routines • Tracking of system response times • Authentication and security data, e.g. encryption keys, passwords
Use	Metadata related to the level and type of use of information resources	• Exhibition records • Use and user tracking • Content re-use and multi-versioning information.

There is a lot of common ground between these two models, and although neither of them specifically mentions 'interoperability' as a purpose, it is alluded to. For instance, Day's Purpose 5 – 'Documenting software and hardware environments' – touches on one aspect of interoperability and the Gilliland-Swetland model refers to technical metadata 'related to how a system functions or metadata behaves'. There is some scope for simplifying Day's model so that 'Preservation management of digital resources' (Purpose 6) becomes part of 'Administration and management of resources' (Purpose 3), a connection that he previously acknowledged (Day, 1999). Likewise 'Providing information on context and authenticity' (Purpose 7) could be grouped with 'Record of intellectual property rights' (Purpose 4) to become 'Record of context, intellectual property rights and authenticity'. Gilliland-Swetland's model could be extended by separating out the description and the information retrieval purposes, for instance.

The five-point model

In this book I propose a new, five-point model to describe the purposes of metadata. It is a closer reflection of current development in metadata and in particular the growing importance of e-commerce. It also separates description from retrieval as a separate, distinct purpose. Some areas have been consolidated such as management of resources and preservation management (which is presented as a sub-set of management) and rights management which is tied in with provenance and authenticity. This model also makes a distinction between the purposes of metadata (i.e. the ways in which it is used) and the intrinsic properties of metadata elements. In doing this it becomes clear that each data element can be used in a variety of ways and fulfils more than one purpose.

The purposes described in the Day and Gilliland-Swetland models can be consolidated into a new, five-point model. The new model encompasses the purposes identified above and includes the additional purposes of interoperability and e-commerce. The five purposes of metadata proposed in this book are described below and provide the basis for later chapters.

1 *Resource description* – This is particularly important in organizations that need to describe their information assets. For example, under the Freedom of Information Act in the UK, public authorities have to produce publication schemes which identify all their publications and intended publications. In the USA, federal agencies have to make information available via the Government Information Locator Service (GILS). These both depend on adequate descriptions of the data. Information asset registers compiled by public authorities and increasingly by the corporate sector also require descriptions of information

repositories and resources.

2 *Information retrieval* – In the academic sector a lot of effort has been put into resource discovery on the internet. Some institutions and agencies have devised subject-based gateways or portals that in effect catalogue relevant high-quality web resources in a particular subject area. This provides users with a route to authoritative sources of information. The cataloguing data usually includes a description of the resource, controlled indexing terms and classification headings. This is a metadata resource and may also 'mine' or 'extract' metadata directly from target websites or electronic resources.

3 *Management of information resources* – The growth of electronic document and records management (EDRM) systems has resulted from the emerging requirements of larger organizations to manage both paper and electronic documentation effectively. EDRM systems need access to 'cataloguing' information about individual documents in order to manage record lifecycles. Examples include authorship, ownership (not necessarily the same thing), provenance of the document (for legal purposes) and date of creation and modification. These and other data elements provide a basis for managing the documentation cost-effectively and consistently. Content management systems (CMSs) are also used to manage data resources including material published on intranets and websites. Chapter 6 describes how metadata is used to manage the retention and disposal of records and the publication of web content in CMS applications.

4 *Documenting ownership and authenticity of digital resources* – Metadata provides a way of declaring the ownership of the intellectual content and layout of a document. It also provides a record of the authenticity of the document by providing an audit trail so that, for instance, an electronic document or a digital image will stand up in court as legally admissible evidence. One of the preconditions for widespread acceptance of electronic documents as original evidence is that electronic systems are becoming the preferred medium for long-term storage of documents.

5 *Interoperability* – Metadata acts as an enabler of information and data transfer between systems, and as such is a key component in interoperability. In order to allow software applications that have been designed independently to pass data between them, a common framework for describing the data being transferred is needed so that each 'knows' how to handle that data in the most appropriate manner. This may be at the level of distinguishing between different languages, or

understanding different data formats.

Interoperability is one of the enablers for e-commerce. When a piece of data is passed from one system to another the accompanying (or embedded) metadata allows the new application to make sense of the data and to use it in the appropriate fashion. This can be seen in the book trade, for instance, where many suppliers using different software packages need to be able to exchange data reliably. The widely adopted ONIX standard allows different participants in the chain from author to reader to exchange data without the need to integrate their systems.

This new five-point model of metadata can be tested by revisiting the reasons for the importance of metadata described earlier. The five functions in the model can be mapped on to the issues as shown in Table 1.2.

Table 1.2   The five-point model and why metadata is important

Why is metadata important?	Purposes of metadata
Retrieval performance	Purpose 1: Resource description
	Purpose 2: Information retrieval
Management of electronic resources	Purpose 3: Resource management
Authenticity	Purpose 4: Ownership and authenticity
Interoperability	Purpose 5: Interoperability
The future	All five purposes

Metadata can be used within one application for several different purposes. The model developed in this chapter helps in the analysis of metadata applications and the understanding of its characteristics in different situations. The five-part model provides the structure for Chapters 4–8 which deal with each purpose of metadata in turn. The next two chapters deal with concepts behind metadata and metadata standards.

summary

Metadata has been around since the first library catalogues were established over 2000 years ago. The term metadata probably first appeared in the 1960s and was adopted by the GIS specialists, database developers, statisticians and latterly, in the 1990s, by the web community.

The term 'metadata' first appeared in the 1960s but became established in the database community in the 1970s. A useful definition sees metadata 'as the means by which the structure and behaviour of data is recorded, controlled, and published across an organization' (Tozer, 1999). This is a useful definition because it does not specify electronic resources and it deals with the key aspects of metadata's purposes.

Some metadata is intended for human readers and some is intended for use by computer applications to help them process or exchange data. Examples of human-readable metadata include web pages with metatags describing the format and content of the resource and a MARC record from a library catalogue. Metadata plays a number of roles including:

- improving retrieval performance
- providing a way of managing electronic resources
- helping to determine the authenticity of data
- enabling interoperability.

Metadata is important because it points to the future of managing information with wider adoption of metadata standards and extensive use in e-commerce.

Different models of metadata have been proposed and a new five-point model is constructed here which describes metadata in terms of the following purposes:

1 Describing information resources
2 Enhancing information retrieval
3 Managing of information resources
4 Documenting ownership and authenticity
5 Exchanging data between systems.

This model reflects current usage of metadata and provides a basis for considering the use of metadata in greater depth. An analysis of the five purposes helps to answer the question 'Why is metadata important?' and gives a framework for the discussion of metadata applications in the later chapters of this book.

References and further sources of information

Bowman, J. H. (2003) *Essential Cataloguing*, London, Facet Publishing.

Caplan, P. (2003) *Metadata Fundamentals for All Librarians*, Chicago, IL, American Library Association.

Day, M. (1999) *Issues and Approaches to Preservation Metadata*. Paper at Joint RLG and NPO Preservation Conference on Guidelines for Digital Imaging, www.rlg.org/preserv/joint/day.html [accessed 25/2/2004I).

Day, M. (2001) Metadata in a Nutshell, *Information Europe*, **6** (2), 11.

Ellens, J. H. (1997) *The Ancient Library of Alexandria: the West's most important repository of learning*, Biblical Review Archives, www.biblereview.org/bswb_AO/brf97library.html [viewed as a cache on Google, 21/1/2004].

Feather, J. and Sturges, P. (eds) (1997) *International Encyclopaedia of Information and Library Science*, London, Routledge.

Gilliland-Swetland, A. (1998) Defining Metadata. In Baca, M. (ed.), *Introduction to Metadata: pathways to digital information*, Los Angeles, CA, Getty Information Institute.

Gorman, M. (2003) *Authority Control in the Context of Bibliographic Control in the Electronic Environment*. Paper at International Conference on Authority Control held in Florence Italy 10–12 February 2003, http://mg.csufresno.edu/papers/Authority_Control.pdf [accessed 25/2/2004].

Hudgins, J., Agnew, G. and Brown, E. (1999) *Getting Mileage out of Metadata: applications for the library*, LITA Guides 5, Chicago, IL, American Library Association.

Hunter, E. J. and Bakewell, K. G. B. (1991) *Cataloguing*, 3rd edn (revised and expanded by E. J. Hunter), London, Library Association Publishing.

ISO 2709:1996. *Information and Documentation – Format for Information Exchange*, Geneva, International Organization for Standardization.

Joint Steering Committee for Revision of AACR (2002a) *A Brief History of AACR*, www.nlc-bnc.ca/jsc/history.html [accessed 24/2/2004].

Joint Steering Committee for the Revision of AACR (2002), American Library Association, Canadian Library Association and CILIP (2000b) *Anglo-American Cataloguing Rules*, 2nd edn, 2002 Revision, Chicago, IL, American Library Association, Ottawa, Canadian Library Association and London, CILIP. Amendments published annually.

Tozer, G. (1999) *Metadata Management for Information Control and Business Success*, Boston, MA, Artech House.

UK Department of Health (n.d.) NSF Diabetes: Delivery Strategy website, www.doh.gov.uk/nsf/diabetes/delivery/foreward.htm [accessed 27/2/2003].

UK Office of the e-Envoy (2001) *E-government Metadata Framework*, London, Office of the e-Envoy.

UK Office of the e-Envoy (2003) *E-government Metadata Standard*, London, Office of the e-Envoy, www.e-envoy.gov.uk/assetRoot/04/00/24/55/04002455.pdf [accessed 25/2/2004].

Vellucci, S. L. (1998) Metadata. In Williams, M. E. (ed.), *Annual Review of Information Science and Technology*, Vol. 33, Medford, NJ, Information Today Inc., 187–222.

Woodley, M. (1999) *Re: History of the term 'metadata'*, Metamarda-l Listserv Archive, 30 March 1999, http://orc.dev.oclc.org:5103/metamarda-l/msg00097.html [accessed 24/5/2004].

Chapter 2
Describing and expressing metadata

overview

THIS CHAPTER SETS out to describe some of the concepts associated with metadata. It considers ways in which metadata can be expressed and focuses on document mark-up languages. It then considers schemas as one method of defining metadata standards and data elements. Databases of metadata are described as an alternative to embedded metadata. One of the key concepts in metadata is the idea of cataloguing data using standard rules and conventions to ensure consistency. This is described in terms of encoding. The last section of the chapter shows some examples of how metadata is used in different contexts such as word-processing, library catalogues, records management, e-commerce and content management systems.

Describing metadata

Although metadata is used in a variety of situations and application areas, its use in documents and specifically in web resources is widespread, human-readable and familiar to many people. For these reasons document mark-up languages have been used here as an example of how to express metadata. The structure of mark-up languages lends them to defining metadata standards through Document Type Definitions (DTDs) and schemas.

Document mark-up

The development of mark-up languages is an excellent example of the way in which metadata can be applied to and expressed in documents. Because documents are widely used and their content is easy to understand, they have the advantage of familiarity when giving examples of metadata use. They are one of the most common forms of digital object to which metadata is applied, and range from web pages to electronic records and on to internal reports and published materials.

Mark-up languages were initially developed to describe the layout and presentation of documents. They enabled organizations to manage large numbers of documents that might need to be presented in a variety of formats. Mark-up languages have provided the means to define metadata associated with documents. This is one of the most powerful ways of embodying metadata associated with documents and is an alternative to database representation of metadata.

Mark-up languages arose from text processing, which is defined as: 'computer systems that can automate parts of the document creation and publishing process' (Goldfarb and Prescod, 2001). Early languages that contained a combination of text and formatting instructions include:

- Troff
- Rich Text Format (RTF)
- LaTeX.

The example in Figure 2.1 shows: raw text (the data), the text with formatting instructions (the rendition) and the text as it would appear to the reader (the presentation). This example uses RTF, but the same principles apply to other rendition notations.

Figure 2.1

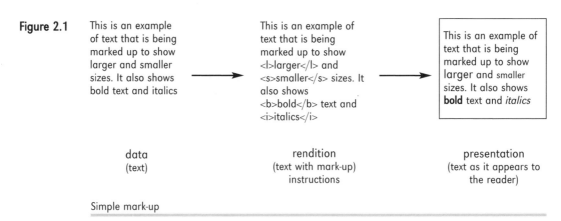

data
(text)

rendition
(text with mark-up)
instructions

presentation
(text as it appears to
the reader)

Simple mark-up

Standard Generalized Mark-up Language

One of the most widely used mark-up languages is Standard Generalized Mark-up Language (SGML), which is used as the basis for describing many web pages and for marking up metadata. Generalized document mark-up originated in the late 1960s from the work of three IBM researchers, Goldfarb, Mosher and Lorie. They determined that a mark-up language would need three attributes:

- Data representation should be common – so that different systems and applications are able to process text in the same representation.
- Mark-up should be extensible – so that it can support all the different types of information that must be exchanged. There is potentially an infinite variety of document types that can be generated.
- Document types need rules – formal rules for documents of a particular type, which can be used to test their conformance to the type and therefore how they are processed.

These attributes provide a framework for representing metadata. A common representation is needed so that metadata elements are clearly identifiable and can be processed appropriately. The extensibility of mark-up languages allows considerable flexibility in creating metadata tags. Document types are used to describe the 'rules' for metadata schemas, so that there is consistency in their expression.

The development of a generalized mark-up language ensured that documents could be handled in a variety of environments. Rather than focusing on formatting instructions, a generalized mark-up language tags different data types. A stylesheet translates generalized mark-up into formatting instructions. For instance, it can instruct a system to represent section headings in bold text and quotations in italics. Different stylesheets can be applied to the same marked-up text. This means that the same text can be presented in different ways, for instance as a printed publication, or displayed as a web page viewed with a browser (see Figure 2.2).

SGML is a long-established international standard, ISO 8879:1986. Hypertext Mark-up Language (HTML) is an application of SGML and Extensible Mark-up Language (XML) is a sub-set of SGML. HTML is used to encode the content of web pages and is widely employed to describe web pages including the metadata embedded in them.

Figure 2.2

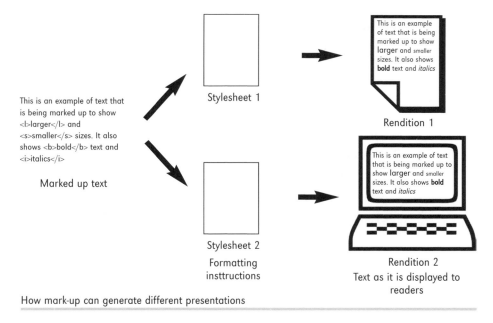

This is an example of text that
is being marked up to show
<l>larger</l> and
<s>smaller</s> sizes. It also
shows bold text and
italics

Marked up text

Stylesheet 1

Rendition 1

Stylesheet 2
Formatting
insttructions

Rendition 2
Text as it is displayed to
readers

How mark-up can generate different presentations

XML

XML (Extensible Mark-up Language)offers the ability to represent data in a simple, flexible, human-readable form. As an open standard, XML is not controlled by one vendor or one country. The XML specifications are published by the World Wide Web Consortium (W3C), an international co-operative venture. XML can be used as a basis for exchange of data or documents between people, computers and applications. It goes further than HTML because it provides a way of expressing a semantic context for data as well as dealing with the syntax. It is the semantic component which gives XML the ability to exchange data in a meaningful way and this is one of the reasons for its widespread uptake as the basis for interoperability.

XML handles content which is made of character data (the text or data content) and mark-up which encodes the logical structure and other attributes of the data. Documents are organized into elements which break the document down into units of meaning, purpose or layout. The elements correspond to fields in a database, as will be seen in later examples in this chapter. XML documents can also use entities, which may refer to an external document or dynamic database record, or which can be used to label a defined piece of text for re-use within the document.

Document Type Definitions (DTDs)

A class of similar documents can be called a 'document type'. A Document Type Definition (DTD) is a set of rules for using XML to represent documents of a particular type. DTDs are an essential component of metadata expression in mark-up languages as they refer to the vocabulary and the rules used to describe metadata.

The DTD defines the elements (or fields) of a document. This means that similar documents can be defined by the same DTD. For instance a memo might have the following elements:

```
To: (the addressee)
From: (the author)
Date: (date on which the memo was sent)
Subject: (what the memo is about)
Body: (the main text of the memo)
```

The DTD for a memo can be used to test the 'validity' of the document. In other words does a document purporting to be a memo have the right elements appearing in the right order? If it does, the DTD provides the means for the memo to be expressed in a variety of formats determined by the appropriate stylesheet. In this example the 'Memo' DTD might have separate stylesheets for printed-out memos, screen displays and e-mail versions.

Carrying on with the memo example, the elements are delimited by tags. The 'To' element could be expressed by the following tags:

```
<To>Jane Williams</To>
```

In this example the start tag <To> is paired with an end tag </To>.

The element may have attributes associated with it – in terms of the encoding system used for instance, or the type of data that appears in that element. For example the 'To' element could be defined by the following statement:

```
<!ELEMENT To (#PCDATA)>
```

This indicates that the 'To' data element consists of Parsed (parsable) Character data (#PCDATA).

Turning to metadata, it is possible to see how DTDs can be used to define the metadata structure of a document. The metadata elements are defined by the DTD. In another hypothetical example of a document type AIM (An Invented Metadata), the AIM schema would be defined by the following DTD:

```
<!ELEMENT AIM (Title, Author, Date)>
<!ELEMENT To (#PCDATA)>
<!ELEMENT From (#PCDATA)>
<!ELEMENT Date (#PCDATA)>
```

In this metadata definition there are three data elements: Title, Author and Date. An example of a document using this DTD would be:

```
<?xml version=3D"1.0"?>
<!DOCTYPE memo SYSTEM "AIM.dtd">
<Title>Describing and Expressing Metadata</Title>
<Author>David Haynes</Author>
<Date>2004-03-22</Date>
```

Schemas

An alternative way of defining metadata is to use XML schemas. They offer greater flexibility than DTDs and are gradually replacing them in XML. Schemas are XML languages used for defining similar types of document in terms of their structure, content and meaning. Schemas can be defined as 'general conceptions of what is common to all members of a class' and are described using XSDL (XML Schema Definition Language). Figure 2.3 is the XML schema that defines simple Dublin Core metadata elements:

Figure 2.3

```
<xs:schema xmlns:xs="http://www.w3.org/2001/XMLSchema"
           xmlns="http://purl.org/dc/elements/1.1/"
           targetNamespace="http://purl.org/dc/elements/1.1/"
           elementFormDefault="qualified"
           attributeFormDefault="unqualified">

 <xs:annotation>
   <xs:documentation xml:lang="en">
    Simple DC XML Schema, 2002-10-09
    by Pete Johnston (p.johnston@ukoln.ac.uk),
    Carl Lagoze (lagoze@cs.cornell.edu), Andy Powell
(a.powell@ukoln.ac.uk),
    Herbert Van de Sompel (hvdsomp@yahoo.com).
    This schema defines terms for Simple Dublin Core, i.e.
    the 15 elements from the http://purl.org/dc/elements/1.1/
    namespace, with no use of encoding schemes or element
    refinements.
    Default content type for all elements is xs:string with
    xml:lang attribute available.

    Supercedes version of 2002-03-12.
    Amended to remove namespace declaration for
http://www.w3.org/XML/1998/namespace namespace,
    and to reference lang attribute via built-in xml:
```

Continued on next page

Figure 2.3
Continued

```
      namespace prefix.
      xs:appinfo also removed.
   </xs:documentation>
 </xs:annotation>

 <xs:import namespace="http://www.w3.org/XML/1998/namespace"
         schemaLocation="http://www.w3.org/2001/03/xml.xsd">
 </xs:import>

 <xs:element name="title" type="elementType"/>
 <xs:element name="creator" type="elementType"/>
 <xs:element name="subject" type="elementType"/>
 <xs:element name="description" type="elementType"/>
 <xs:element name="publisher" type="elementType"/>
 <xs:element name="contributor" type="elementType"/>
 <xs:element name="date" type="elementType"/>
 <xs:element name="type" type="elementType"/>
 <xs:element name="format" type="elementType"/>
 <xs:element name="identifier" type="elementType"/>
 <xs:element name="source" type="elementType"/>
 <xs:element name="language" type="elementType"/>
 <xs:element name="relation" type="elementType"/>
 <xs:element name="coverage" type="elementType"/>
 <xs:element name="rights" type="elementType"/>

 <xs:group name="elementsGroup">
 <xs:sequence>
   <xs:choice minOccurs="0" maxOccurs="unbounded">
    <xs:element ref="title"/>
    <xs:element ref="creator"/>
    <xs:element ref="subject"/>
    <xs:element ref="description"/>
    <xs:element ref="publisher"/>
    <xs:element ref="contributor"/>
    <xs:element ref="date"/>
    <xs:element ref="type"/>
    <xs:element ref="format"/>
    <xs:element ref="identifier"/>
    <xs:element ref="source"/>
    <xs:element ref="language"/>
    <xs:element ref="relation"/>
    <xs:element ref="coverage"/>
    <xs:element ref="rights"/>
  </xs:choice>
  </xs:sequence>
 </xs:group>

 <xs:complexType name="elementType">
   <xs:simpleContent>
    <xs:extension base="xs:string">
     <xs:attribute ref="xml:lang" use="optional"/>
    </xs:extension>
   </xs:simpleContent>
 </xs:complexType>

</xs:schema>
```

The XML schema that defines simple Dublin Core metadata elements (Johnston et al., 2002)

The start of the schema contains declarations about the nature of the schema, including two namespace references 'xmlns' (see below). This is followed by some annotations by the authors about the background to the schema and then a namespace reference to the standard for XML. Namespace declarations can also be used to link to a metadata standard or encoding scheme at the start of a record. The main body of the schema defines the 15 data elements in simple Dublin Core, followed by a declaration of the sequence or order in which the data elements would normally appear.

Schemas are commonly associated with databases, where each data element corresponds to a field in a database. As with databases the schema can be set up to provide semantic and syntactic checks on data. In other words checks on the meaning and grammar of an expression can be made. Syntactic checks, for example, can be applied to the data to ensure that it is of the appropriate type and is expressed in a format that can be processed by the database software. For instance, dates can be defined using international standard ISO 8601:2000 to get over the problem of differing American and British date order, which can look the same but have different meanings. For example 10/12/02 means 10 December 2002 in the UK and October 12, 2002 in the USA. They can also apply semantic checks to ensure that business rules are followed – for instance by requiring the value of an element (the field content) to fall within a specified range.

Namespace

Namespace is used to locate definitions for metadata schema from the internet. This ensures greater consistency of terminology used to define metadata elements and provides a way of sharing elements. In the Dublin Core example the namespace that provides the original reference to Dublin core elements is as follows:

```
xmlns="http://purl.org/dc/elements/1.1"
```

A formal definition is:

An **XML namespace** is a collection of names, identified by a URI reference, which are used in XML documents as element types and attribute names.

(W3C, 2003)

Databases of metadata

The previous section about the mark-up of documents focused particularly on embedded metadata. For example a web resource may have metadata tags and content embedded in the resource. Electronic documents often have metadata attached to them, allowing other applications and systems to effectively process them. However this is not the only way of handling metadata. In many systems the metadata associated with an information object may be held centrally in a database of metadata. Sometimes the term 'metadatabase' is used, but this can be ambiguous: certain communities such as those concerned with biodiversity and geographical information systems use the term 'metadatabase' for a database of databases, pointing to data collections from several sources. There is of course some overlap in meaning, because some metadata may be about databases rather than other resources.

Examples of databases of metadata include content management systems (CMSs), Electronic Document and Records Management (EDRM) systems and subject-based gateways. For instance content management systems store the metadata about web (or intranet) resources in a central database and use this data to process the resources. They bring up material due for review, manage the workflow, and control access by limiting it to authorized users. In records management, EDRM systems work with central repositories of metadata, allowing records to be managed more effectively. They identify when records are due for disposal, and what level of security is appropriate for them. Databases of metadata are also used for retrieval. The JISC-funded Resource Discovery Network (www.rdn.ac.uk) provides access to specialist subject-based gateways that are effectively specialist databases (or catalogues) of metadata about selected web resources that have been evaluated for quality and relevance. A searcher interested in 'tax law', for instance, can enter the term into the SOSIG (Social Science Information Gateway) which specializes in social science, business and law, and will be referred to 19 high-quality web resources that are of direct relevance out of a database of 50,000 items.

How to catalogue data

Metadata is used to improve the utility of data by providing a structure or framework for describing that data. The earlier description of DTDs and schemas showed how the data elements that make up the metadata are defined and the sequence or order in which these data elements should appear. However the examples that were considered did not go into detail about the way in which the metadata is encoded.

Data elements and encoding metadata

Metadata elements are in effect fields of information that can be stored and manipulated in a database or a spreadsheet (as in a library catalogue or other metadatabase). Alternatively the data elements may be embedded in a document, delimited by tags. The marked-up metadata tags may also include details of the metadata schema used and the encoding system that has been adopted.

For example, the Library of Congress uses generic metadata tags to declare the content of the data element 'description', but does not indicate which language, authority file or encoding scheme is used for the content:

```
<meta name="description" content="The Library of
Congress Home Page.">
```

However in the next example, from the British Library home page, the DC.Identifier data element indicates an encoding scheme. This in effect tells the reader (or application) that the content of the data field is a uniform resource identifier (URI). In this case the content is the web address of the British Library's home page.

```
<meta name="DC.Identifier" scheme="URI"
content="http://www.bl.uk/ index.shtml">
```

Another example can be seen from the National Library of Australia's home page:

```
<META NAME="DC.Identifier" SCHEME="URI" CONTENT=
"http://www.nla.gov.au">
```

Both of the above websites use the Dublin Core Metadata Element Set (DCMES), which is described in more detail in Chapter 3, pp 51–3. The name of the data element is declared by the phrase: 'meta name=', the actual name of the data element is surrounded in double quotes, in this case "DC.Identifier". The actual metadata content is declared by the phrase 'content=', and the actual data is again surrounded in double quotes; in these cases they are the URIs for the two websites.

Expressing metadata

Data can be catalogued in a variety of ways, as demonstrated by some of the examples described here. Common applications such as word-processors, electronic document and records management systems, library catalogues and e-commerce applications all make extensive use of metadata. Some of these application areas are covered more fully in the chapters about the specific purposes of metadata.

Word documents

Word-processing packages often automatically create metadata when a document is saved for the first time. In some cases the author of the document may be invited to add metadata as the document is being saved. For example, Microsoft Word can be configured to prompt the author for metadata when a new document is being saved for the first time. Some metadata, such as title, author and company, is automatically generated. These can be edited and additional metadata can be created for subject, manager, category, keywords and comments. This is a useful way of ensuring consistent retrieval of documents. Keywords that do not appear in the text of the document can be added as metadata to enrich the subject description of the document.

The screenshot in Figure 2.4 shows a typical metadata screen as seen in a Microsoft Word document. The other tabs – 'General', 'Statistics' and 'Contents' – display metadata such as document size, time spent editing it, the session number and the number of words. This is generated by the software. The final tab, 'Custom', allows for additional optional data associated with document and records management. This metadata feature is accessible in Microsoft Word via the File–Properties menu.

Electronic records management

The word-processing example has shown metadata designed for human use and often requiring human intervention. However metadata is increasingly used by computer applications without direct human intervention. Electronic Document and Records Management (EDRM) systems make use of metadata associated with documents to manage them effectively. While many of these data elements can be examined by human beings, they are used by computer applications to process records during their lifecycles.

An example of this is the retention period of a document or record. It is current practice (ISO 15489:2001) for records to be assigned a specific category according to a file plan (usually a business classification scheme applied to an organization's records). Typically each category in the file plan will have a set retention period. For exam-

Metadata for Information Management and Retrieval

Example of metadata associated with a document created in Microsoft Word™
Screen shot reprinted by permission from Microsoft Corporation

ple in a recruitment process, interview records may be kept for six months from the interview date before disposal (unless the candidate is successfully recruited). Invoices may be kept for six years on the other hand. The file category is one piece of metadata associated with a record, used by the EDRM system to identify records that are due for review or disposal at the end of the appropriate retention period. In order to do this the system will have to call on another metadata element containing information on the date created. EDRM systems use this metadata to generate a disposal list for review by a records manager or administrator.

Library catalogues

Metadata is particularly useful for large collections of documents or other materials, where it can be used for managing the resource and for finding specific items. A catalogue becomes an essential tool for retrieval when there are more than a few hundred items in a library. The arrangement of books in a subject classification is not always sufficient for good subject retrieval. In response to this need, librarians have developed metadata which is captured in a catalogue. Early examples of library metadata were held on catalogue cards. In the 1960s electronic catalogues began to appear and these are routinely used in most libraries today. Library users or patrons can find books by searching the catalogue or OPAC (online public access catalogue) by a variety of criteria such as author name, words in the title, classification code (which determines the arrangement on the shelves) and keyword (subject). This is not an exhaustive list, but demonstrates the role played by metadata in a library catalogue, by providing a variety of search options for the retrieval of items.

Figure 2.5 is an example of a catalogue record from the Geac system used in the City of Westminster Libraries in London. A search on the author name 'Doyle' retrieved 1002 items of which a significant number belong to the Sherlock Holmes Collection in the Marylebone Library of Westminster City Council near Baker Street in London. Baker Street is a real location within the City of Westminster where the fictitious character Sherlock Holmes lived. The subject field contains the entry 'Doyle, Sir Arthur Conan, 1859–1930', which is probably from a name authority file. Without this structured data about books in Westminster City Libraries it would be much more difficult to locate individual titles. In this example the metadata is used to store comparable data about individual items in the collection. This allows users to search consistently across the whole collection.

Searching a group of catalogues

It is also possible to search across a group of library catalogues (working like a virtual union catalogue). Metadata allows users to structure data from different resources so that it is possible to simultaneously search across several resources at once. For example the M25 Consortium of Academic Libraries in and around London provides access to all the members' catalogues simultaneously through its InforM25 Service. Use of a common protocol, Z39.50 (ANSI/NISO 239.50), allows interoperability between the catalogues. It maps existing metadata terms to 'attribute sets'. The Z39.50 standard is being updated to take into account XML and web-service protocols such as SOAP (Mitra, 2003) in a group of initiatives is known as ZING – Z39.50 International: Next Generation. Common cataloguing rules such as AACR2 help to ensure each element

Figure 2.5

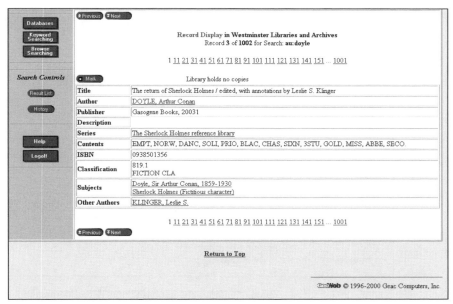

Example of a catalogue record from Westminster City Libraries

is comparable between systems, so that, for instance, the author name always takes the form Surname, First Name.

The search example in Figure 2.6 shows the benefit of consistent cataloguing. A simple search for books with the word 'Metadata' in the title yields the result shown in Figure 2.7. The system allows users to view details of individual titles found at each institution.

The search results reveal that there are eleven books on metadata at University College London (UCL), nine at the University of Greenwich, seven at the University of Reading and four each in Kingston University and the London School of Economics. All of this is possible because of the structured metadata and the consistent cataloguing rules that allow searching across resources.

E-commerce

E-commerce systems make extensive use of metadata. The book trade provides a good example of how different parts of the supply chain interact using metadata. For example, a book retailer may place an order with a publisher for a certain quantity of its titles to be delivered to a specific location by a particular date. The order will contain metadata elements describing the books on order. The order itself will contain additional metadata that can be used to authenticate it. This helps the supplier to answer

Figure 2.6

Search screen from the InforM25 Service

Figure 2.7

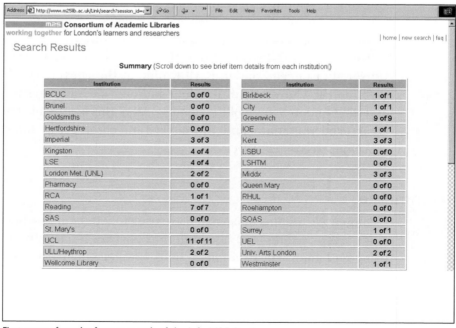

First page of results from a search of the InforM25 Service

Metadata for Information Management and Retrieval

the following questions: 'Is this a genuine order?', 'When was it generated?', 'Who validated it?', and so forth. Bringing these strands together the electronic order results in the exchange of metadata about the book between the retailer and the publisher. Rights data for payment of royalties and any special offers or conditions of sale is also exchanged. This will then trigger a financial transaction that transfers funds between the bank accounts of the two organizations.

In the example of the product record in Figure 2.8, as well as biblio-

Figure 2.8

```
<product>
        <a001>1234567890</a001>
        <a002>03</a002>
        <b004>0816016356</b004>
        <b012>BB</b012>
        <b028>British English, A to Zed</b028>
        <contributor>
        <b035>A01</b035>
        <b037>Schur, Norman W</b037>
        <b044>A Harvard graduate in Latin and Italian literature, Norman Schur attended
        the University of Rome and the Sorbonne before returning to the United States to
        study law at Harvard and Columbia Law Schools. Now retired from legal practice,
        Mr Schur is a fluent speaker and writer of both British and American English
        </b044>
        </contributor>
        <b056>REV</b056>
        <b057>3</b057>
        <b059>eng</b059>
        <b061>493</b061>
        <b064>REF008000</b064>
        <b073>01</b073>
        <b079>Facts on File Publications</b079>
        <b081>Facts on File Inc</b081>
        <b003>1987</b003>
        <c096>9.25</c096>
        <c097>6.25</c097>
        <c098>1.2</c098>
        <d101>BRITISH ENGLISH, A TO ZED is the thoroughly updated, revised, and
        expanded third edition of Norman Schur's highly acclaimed transatlantic
        dictionary for English speakers. First published as BRITISH SELF-TAUGHT and
        then as ENGLISH ENGLISH, this collection of Briticisms for Americans, and
        Americanisms for the British, is a scholarly yet witty lexicon, combining definitions
        with commentary on the most frequently used and some lesser known words and
        phrases. Highly readable, it's a snip of a book, and one that sorts out – through
        comments in American – the "Queen's English" – confounding as it may
        seem.</d101>
        <e110>Norman Schur is without doubt the outstanding authority on the similarities
        and differences between British and American English. BRITISH ENGLISH, A TO
        ZED attests not only to his expertise, but also to his undiminished powers to inform,
        amuse and entertain. – Laurence Urdang, Editor, VERBATIM, The Language
        Quarterly, Spring 1988 </e110>
        <supplydetail>
        <j136>1234567</j136>
        <j141>IP</j141>
        <price>
        <j148>01</j148>
        <j151>35.00</j151>
        </price>
        </supplydetail>
</product>
```

Product record example (from: http://libraries.mit.edu/guides/subjects/metadata/standards/onix.html)

graphic information, there is promotional text about the author and the publication, details of price, and the scope to add other information under 'supply detail'.

Content management systems

Content management systems (CMSs) are widely used for managing the content of large websites, although they can be used for managing content in other environments. Boiko (2002) sees metadata as an essential component of content management systems:

> Computers are designed to deal with data that's stripped of any context and independent meaning. Users want computers to deal with content, however, which is rich in context and meaning. The compromise . . . is to wrap your information in a data container (known as metadata).

Content management systems can have an extensive range of functions, but they are all able to help with the collection, management and publication of content. The content may be document based, or it can be dynamically generated from a database. It can be presented in a number of different formats. The accompanying metadata helps the CMS to capture the content in the appropriate way. Additional metadata may be generated that establishes where the content came from, who can have access to it, the renewal dates, who is responsible for the content, and subject keywords and categories to describe the content.

CMSs are not limited to websites and are increasingly being used as a way of providing access to a repository of information resources via a number of different delivery channels such as a customer call system, digital TV, intranets (for internal users) and the internet (for the public). For more on these systems see Chapter 7.

summary

Document mark-up languages such as SGML and its subset XML can be used to define metadata through Document Type Definitions (DTDs) and schemas. They can also be used to express metadata, particularly in a web resource. One of the features of XML is its ability to present documents or data in a way that can be read directly by humans but which can also be processed by computer applications. It forms the basis for interoperability and its flexibility has led to widespread adoption by specialist communities. An alternative to mark-up languages is to establish databases of metadata, which is the approach typically used for library catalogues.

Metadata is used in a variety of contexts including word-processing, library catalogues, virtual union catalogues, electronic records management, e-commerce and content management systems.

This sets the scene for a discussion of information models and metadata standards, the subject of Chapter 3.

References and further sources of information

ANSI/NISO Z39.50 – 2003. Information Retrieval: Application Service Definition and Protocol Specification, Bethesda, MD, National Information Standards Organization, www.niso.org/standards/dtandard_detail.cfm?std_id=465 [accessed 26/2/2004].

Boiko, B. (2002) *Content Management Bible*, New York, NY, Wiley Publishing Inc.

Goldfarb, C. F. and Prescod, P. (2001) *The XML Handbook*, 3rd edn, Upper Saddle River, NJ, Prentice Hall.

ISO 8879:1986. *Standard Generalized Markup Language*, Geneva, International Organization for Standardization.

ISO 8601:2000. *Data Elements and Interchange Formats – Information Exchange – Representations of Dates and Times*, Geneva, International Organization for Standardization.

ISO 15489:2001. *Information and Documentation – Records Management*, Geneva, International Organization for Standardization.

Johnson, P., Lagoze, C., Powell, A. and Van de Sompel, H. (2002) *Simple DC XML Schema*, Version 2002-12-12, Dublin Core Metadata Initiative, http://dublincore.org/schemas/xmls/simpledc20021212.xsd [accessed 26/2/2004].

Mitra, N. (ed.) (2003) *SOAP Versions 1.2 Part 0: Primer. W3C Recommendation*, www.w3.org/TR/2003/REC-soap12-part0-20030624/ [accessed 26/2/2004].

UK Office of the e-Envoy (2003) *E-government Metadata Standard with XML Syntax*, Version 2.0, London, UK Cabinet Office.

W3C (2003) *XML Namespace*, www.w3c.org/TR/REC-xml-names/ [accessed 21/4/2003].

ZING Homepage, www.loc.gov/z3950/a [accessed 26/2/2004].

Chapter 3
Standards and data models

overview

THIS CHAPTER CONSIDERS some of the metadata models currently in use to gain an understanding of the development of metadata standards. It focuses on standards that are widely used or which have the promise of becoming widely adopted. There are distinct communities of interest which are developing their own common frameworks and standards for metadata and the chapter concentrates on those of direct relevance to the library, information and records management fields. It also covers standards for web resources and multimedia.

In order to understand metadata schemes and standards, the chapter reviews some of the data modelling systems which have been developed to analyse data elements and the relationships between them. This is followed by a discussion of the characteristics of different types of standard illustrated by examples of the main metadata standards as well as schemes and application profiles that are not formal standards. The standards have been grouped according to communities of interest, such as the web community, cultural heritage, publishing, multimedia, education and government sectors. A more detailed description of the way some of these standards and schemas are used is given in later chapters that deal with specific metadata application areas. The chapter covers both international and national metadata schemes and standards.

Metadata models

A metadata standard is in effect a data model. The model may have its own syntax and semantics and will therefore have some of the features of a mark-up language such as XML. One of the interesting characteristics of recent metadata development has been the convergence of different communities of interest that have developed their own metadata standards. Different groups are beginning to see the benefits and advantages of working within common frameworks. In order to do so they have to develop common languages for describing the data that they handle. Languages such as XML and models such as RDF have played an important role in equipping these communities with a set of tools to analyse data and relationships between data elements.

This chapter introduces several widely used systems including the ABC Ontology, and the Resource Description Framework (RDF), which are both examples of ontology – defining languages. The chapter also describes the Functional Requirements for Bibliographic Records (FRBR) and the Indecs metadata framework used for intellectual property rights, which are both examples of ontologies for specific domains.

Ontologies

There is a lot of confusion about where ontologies fit in the domain of taxonomies and classification systems. A general definition of an ontology is: 'an explicit formal specification of how to represent the objects, concepts and other entities that are assumed to exist in some area of interest and the relationships that hold among them' (International DOI Foundation, 2003). An ontology is a way of modelling reality and as such is a knowledge representation. A recent article (McGuinness, 2002) describes three universal properties of all ontologies: (i) a finite controlled vocabulary; (ii) unambiguous interpretation of classes and term relationships; and (iii) strict hierarchical sub-class relationships between classes. In effect an ontology takes the form of a specialist type of classification system or taxonomy. McGuinness goes on to describe uses of ontologies and in particular their application in a web environment. These range from being a source of controlled vocabulary, to a way of organizing content, to improvement of navigation, browsing and retrieval capabilities. More complex ontologies can be used for modelling data.

ABC Ontology

The ABC Ontology is 'a basic model and ontology that provides the notional basis for developing domain, role or community specific ontologies' (Lagoze and Hunter, 2001). The model is intended to provide a basis for analysing existing metadata ontologies, to give communities the tools to develop their own ontologies and to provide a mechanism for mapping between metadata ontologies.

The ABC Ontology was developed to facilitate interoperability between metadata ontologies from different domains. Its target is to 'model physical, digital and analogue objects held in libraries, archives and museums and on the Internet' (Lagoze and Hunter, 2001). This includes books, museum objects, digital images, sound recordings and multimedia resources. It can model abstract concepts such as intellectual content, time-based events such as a performance, or a lifecycle event that happens to an object such as the publication of a book. The model is based on a primitive category 'Entity' with three categories at the next level: Temporality, Actuality and Abstraction. The data elements used for each category are:

- ENTITY
  - Time
  - Place
- TEMPORALITY
  - Situation
  - Event
  - Action
- ACTUALITY
  - Artifact
  - Agent
- ABSTRACTION
  - Work.

Each category has sub-categories that allow for more precise descriptions of the models. These in turn can be broken down into sub-classes specific to a particular domain, such as libraries, museums, web resources, and so on. The ABC Ontology allows for modelling of time-dependent relationships which are particularly important in museums and archives (where the provenance of an item is integral to its integrity), and for rights management where it may be important to track who has used a work under what conditions and when.

Figure 3.1 is a simplified representation of a publication using the ABC Ontology. The Work *Omeros* is manifest as a book which was authored by the Nobel Laureate Derek Walcott in 1990 and was subsequently published by Faber and Faber in the same year. A more complete representation of this would indicate the place of publication and co-publishing details.

One consequence of the sophistication of the ABC Ontology, which allows for complex modelling of entities and the relationships between them, is the considerable effort required to analyse elements and rela-

Figure 3.1

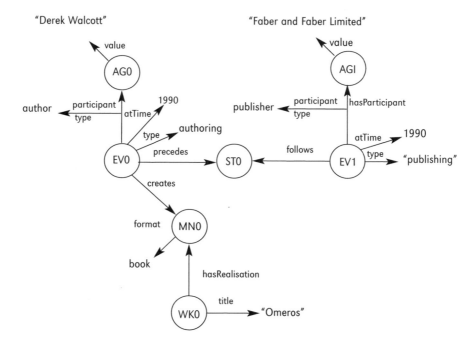

Using ABC Ontology to represent a publication

tionships. It therefore only becomes worthwhile if the resulting benefits are sufficiently large, as in e-commerce applications.

Resource Description Framework

RDF is a language for representing information about resources on the internet (Manola and Miller, 2004). It was one of the first tools developed for modelling and describing web resources. It goes beyond metadata description by providing a model for the relationships between different metadata elements. It bridges the divide between human-generated and machine-generated (and processed) metadata and works with different types of object or data entities.

RDF can be expressed in mark-up languages such as HTML and XML. Its purpose is to enable the encoding, exchange and re-use of metadata definitions or schema. The system is flexible, allowing each resource description community to define its own metadata elements. It also allows those communities to tap into existing schema and to re-use elements that may be relevant to their situation. The namespace convention ensures that there is a unique reference back to the original definition. This system exploits the power and range of the internet and avoids the need for a central register or repository of data elements. As an object-oriented system RDF is based on three object types:

- *Resources* – anything being described by RDF expressions. This could be a web page or a printed book, for instance.
- *Properties* – an attribute or characteristic of the resource being described. For instance 'Creator' can be applied to a web page, or 'Author' can be a property of a book. The schema specification will describe how that property is expressed. For instance, cataloguing rules may require authors to take the form: Surname, initials. Thus the author Jane Smith would be expressed as 'Smith, J'.
- *Statements* – a statement applies to a specific resource and includes a subject (the resource), the predicate (the property) and object (the value of the property).

The statement syntax subject–predicate–object is known as a triple or 3-tuple. For instance the following statement describes the author of a book and can be represented by the triple:

Arthur Conan Doyle (object, or property) is the creator (predicate, or property type) of the book, Hound of the Baskervilles (subject, or resource)

This statement can be represented by a node and arc diagram (Figure 3.2), which groups together a resource (node) linked by a property type (arc) to a value.

This structure is recursive, so that an object may itself be a statement. That statement's object may itself be a statement. An example of this more complex relationship is shown in Figure 3.3. The author name is represented by an ID number with properties of 'Name' and 'Lifespan' associated with it. In the 'node and arc' diagram in Figure 3.3 the object of the statement is itself a statement. 'The Hound of the Baskervilles has creator . . .'

Figure 3.2

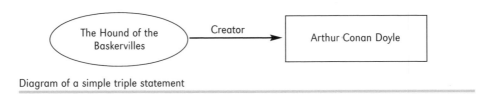

Diagram of a simple triple statement

Figure 3.3

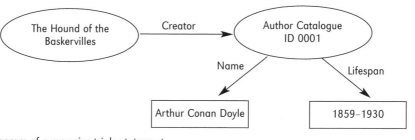

Diagram of a recursive triple statement

leads to the statement 'Author Catalogue ID 0001 has name Arthur Conan Doyle and has lifespan 1859–1930'.

Looking at the construction of an RDF statement expressed in XML syntax helps to show the way in which RDF works. In this example the RDF container is surrounded by a pair of tags, opening with:

```
<rdf:RDF
```

and closing with:

```
</rdf:RDF>
```

The opening rdf statement includes the RDF namespace declaration, which refers to the specific URI where the rdf definition in XML is held. This allows multiple and consistent use of XML resources, because different documents can refer to the same namespace. It also ensures that an application can recognize and use the appropriate version of RDF to interpret the statements that follow.

```
<rdf:RDF xmlns:
rdf="http://www.w3.org/1999/02/22-rdf-syntax-ns#"
```

The following pair of tags is used to create a container element for each resource being described:

```
<rdf:Description
</rdf:Description>
```

In the first example the author is declared (we have used the Dublin Core schema described later in this chapter (pp 51–3) to define the data elements) in the following statement:

```
<rdf:Description rdf:about="The Hound of the
Baskervilles">
        <dc:creator>Arthur Conan Doyle</dc:creator>
</rdf:Description>
```

Further information about RDF can be found at the W3C website
(www.w3.org/TR/2004/rdf-primer/).

Functional Requirements for Bibliographic Records

Functional Requirements for Bibliographic Records (FRBR) is a system
for modelling bibliographic information associated with monographs,
recordings and museum objects. It is capable of modelling about 1200 entities and relationships, which is around half the number of data elements
defined in MARC. FRBR arose from the Paris Principles for cataloguing
agreed in 1961 and the ISBDs (International Standard Bibliographic
Descriptions) that followed the Copenhagen meeting of cataloguing
experts in 1969 (IFLA, 1998). FRBR models the functions performed by
bibliographic records and covers various media, different applications and
a range of user needs. The model defines relationships between entities
which have particular attributes. Entities are 'key objects of interest to
users of bibliographic data' (IFLA, 1998) and can be *products* of intellectual work or artistic creation; they may be the *subject* of that intellectual
or artistic work, or they may be the entities *responsible* for the work. For
instance, the book *Wonderful Life* is a work on the subject 'evolutionary
development' or, more specifically, 'the Cambrian explosion', and the person 'Stephen J. Gould' is responsible for its creation; in other words he
is the author.

Another example is the choral work 'Die Schöpfung', a product of
'Joseph Haydn' who was responsible for composing the musical work,
which is known in English as 'The Creation'.

The entities can be defined more specifically. For example a product
can be defined as:

- Work – a distinct intellectual or artistic creation
- Expression – intellectual or artistic realization of a work
- Manifestation – physical embodiment of an expression of a work
- Item – single exemplar of a manifestation.

In the example above, 'Die Schöpfung' is a *Work*. The performance of that work by Leonard Bernstein recorded by Polydor International in 1987 is an *Expression* of that work and the two-CD set released by Deutsche Grammophon is the *Manifestation* of that expression of the work. The particular CD set in a collection of CDs is an *Item*.

Responsible entities can be people, groups of people or organizations. The types of responsibility are defined by different relationships. For instance Joseph Haydn as composer has one type of relationship to the work, but Leonard Bernstein the conductor is responsible for its expression, as is Polydor International, the organization that made the recording and Deutsche Grammophon which published the manifestation.

Figures 3.4 and 3.5 show the relationship between different product entities and entities responsible for an intellectual or artistic creation. The double-headed arrows indicate that there may be multiple instances of a relationship between entities. The relationships are directional, going left to right and from top to bottom. For instance a work *is created by* a person (or persons). The reverse relationship is that a person *creates* a work (or works).

Figure 3.4 illustrates the relationships between a Work, an Expression, a Manifestation and an Item. It also shows in general terms the relationship between a product and the responsible person or corporate body.

Figure 3.5 shows how a subject may be related to a work. The subject of a work may be a product, a responsible entity or a subject. A work may be about more than one subject, and a subject may have more than one

Figure 3.4

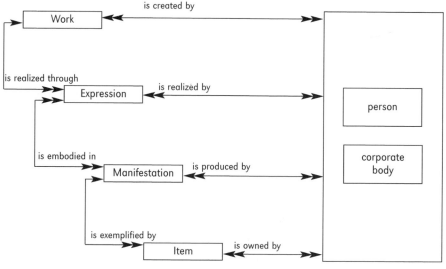

FRBR model of relationships between product and creative entities

Figure 3.5

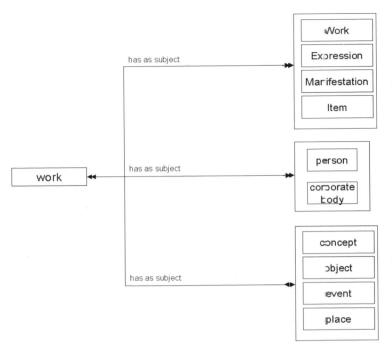

FRBR model of relationships between product and and subject entities

work about it. This many-to-many relationship is indicated by the double-headed arrows.

The entities illustrated in these diagrams have properties or attributes, which are equivalent to data elements or fields. For example a work may have attributes such as title or date associated with it.

The FRBR model provides a way of analysing bibliographic entities. This is having a profound effect on cataloguing practice, so that, for instance, the common bibliographic elements of different expressions of a work will be catalogued only once at work level and the same basic record will be refined with additional fields that apply at expression, manifestation and item level. The *Anglo-American Cataloguing Rules* (Joint Steering Committee for the Revision of AACR, 2002) are being rewritten to fit into the FRBR framework, so that AACR3 will use the FRBR data model.

Indecs metadata framework

The Indecs metadata framework was developed to provide a basis for interoperability of e-commerce systems, especially those related to intellectual property items such as music recordings, written work or museum artefacts.

Indecs is used to identify and describe items from different data sources. Its use has been incorporated into sectoral standards such as ONIX and DOI (see p 70). Indecs is a model for commerce (Rust and Bide, 2000). The framework centres on four axioms about e-commerce:

1 *Metadata is critical* – In order to trade electronically you need information about who is trading, what is being traded and the nature of the transaction. These are all metadata. A common understanding of the metadata elements is necessary for a successful transaction to take place.
2 *Stuff is complex* – An item such as a recording may have many separate pieces that each carries its own rights. For instance a recording of a piece of music on a CD may have rights associated with the composer, the publisher, the conductor, the performers, the recording studio, the text used for the sleeve notes and any illustrations that are used for the cover.
3 *Metadata is modular* – Each entity must have its own metadata, even if they are part of a larger item, if the rights associated with them are to be protected. The modules are linked together as a metadata network.
4 *Transactions need automation* – For e-commerce to work, it is important that local data standards and systems are standardized. This opens the way for the automation of rights transactions and makes it possible to handle the very large volume of requests that would come in to a rights holder.

The Indecs framework has defined metadata elements, each of which has an Indecs identifier or iid. The Indecs framework can be used to model the relationships between entities. Indecs is based on the premises that: 'People make stuff', 'People use stuff' and 'People do deals about stuff'. This is shown in Figure 3.6.

More complex models can be developed to reflect detailed transactions and to represent the intellectual property rights associated with works, known as 'stuff' in the model. This modelling tool forms the basis of ONIX, an e-commerce system for the publishing industry which is covered later in this chapter (pp 57–9) and described in greater detail in Chapter 7 (pp 122–3).

Figure 3.6

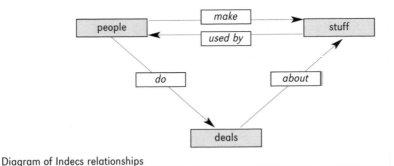

Diagram of Indecs relationships

Open Archival Information Standard

The Open Archival Information Standard (OAIS) was developed to provide a functional and information model of information preservation for access and use by a designated community of consumers. The OAIS model encompasses a range of information, from that which is regularly updated to that which has periodic updates, and from simple access systems to sophisticated access systems and deals with the highly distributed nature of many information systems. The simple model (Figure 3.7) is based on the idea that information from a producer is input to the OAIS archive which is managed and provides output for consumers such as the designated community that it was intended for.

The information is packaged with a wrapper of package information about which description information is available (see Figure 3.8). The package contains Content Information and Preservation Description Information (PDI). The PDI has a number of attributes:

- *Provenance* – source of the content information, including its custody and history
- *Context* – relationship of the content to other information outside the package
- *Reference* – identifiers such as ISBNs (for books)

Figure 3.7

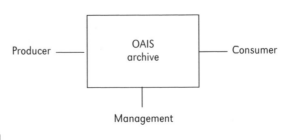

Simple OAIS model

Figure 3.8

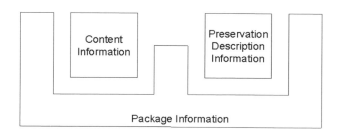

OAIS wrapper of package information

- *Fixity* – which provides protection against undocumented alteration, e.g. check sum.

A slightly more complex representation of the OAIS model can be seen in Figure 3.9, although this is still a high-level representation. The Submission Information Package (SIP) is sent by the Producer to an OAIS archive. It will contain some content and some PDI. One or more SIPs are transformed into an Archival Information Package (AIP) which conforms to the internal architecture of the OAIS archive. It will have a complete set of PDI for the Content Information. When a consumer makes a request for information the OAIS will produce a Dissemination Information Package (DIP) in response.

Figure 3.9

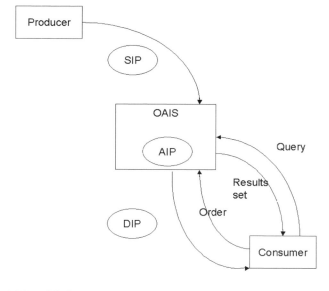

OAIS model of a query

A fuller description of OAIS can be found in the *Reference Model for an Open Archival Information System* (Consultative Committee for Space Data Systems, 2002).

About standards

What is a standard?

There is some confusion about what a standard is and the difference between metadata standards, schemas and application profiles. It helps to go back to definitions of standards to get a better understanding of these different concepts.

A standard is a common specification for a product, system or method that ensures consistent performance within agreed limits. ISO, the International Organization for Standardization, defines a standard as follows:

> Standards are documented agreements containing technical specifications or other precise criteria to be used consistently as rules, guidelines, or definitions of characteristics, to ensure that materials, products, processes and services are fit for their purpose.
>
> (International Organization for Standardization, 2002)

There are different types of standard which can be listed in order of increasing formality as:

- *proprietary standards* – developed by a supplier and applying to its products
- *de facto standards* – standards which have become widely used and accepted without going through the formal standardization process
- *industry standards* – developed around a specific industry or sector and often international in scope
- *national and regional standards* – standards set by official national bodies such as ANSI, BSI or regional bodies such as CEN and CENELEC
- *international standards* – standards issued by one of the three international bodies.

National and international standards are examples of *de jure* standards and are in contrast to the *de facto* standards that have grown up in different sectors. Metadata standards fall into all of the above categories and examples will be seen throughout this book. This chapter concentrates on international standards and industry standards that transcend national boundaries.

National and international standards are the most formal standards, with set procedures for standards development. At the international level there are three standards bodies: ISO, the International Organization for Standardization; ITU, the International Telecommunication Union; and IEC, the International Electrotechnical Commission. Their roles are broadly complementary: the ITU concentrates on telecommunications and radio communications technologies; the IEC deals with electrical and electronic engineering technologies; and everything else is covered by ISO. However, there is some overlap between them, particularly in the area of information technology and management where the bodies work together by means of joint committees and co-ordinating groups.

Internal standards and proprietary standards may of course be less formal than this in their development, but similar principles will apply. Bodies such as ISO sometimes fast-track existing standards created by other bodies so that the earlier drafting stages are skipped and they go straight to committee stage.

Metadata standards

Metadata standards have evolved to suit the needs of different communities of interest or industry sectors. Key factors influencing their development have been business needs, user groups, and the history or legacy of particular communities. This section considers some of the most commonly used standards for the web, libraries, archives, publishing, multimedia and education.

Dublin Core and the web community

Early pioneers of the world wide web became concerned about the difficulty of finding resources on the internet. In 1995 a meeting was held in Dublin, Ohio, to discuss ways of describing and categorizing web content. This led to the formation of the Dublin Core Metadata Initiative (DCMI) 'an organization dedicated to promoting the widespread adoption of interoperable metadata standards and developing specialized metadata vocabularies for describing resources that enable more intelligent information discovery systems' (DCMI, 2004). It is a collaborative effort with participants from around the world and with a range of backgrounds, and relies on the co-operative efforts of individuals and organizations. The

Dublin Core is one of the most widely used metadata standards and has become the basis for more specialist spin-offs such as the UK government's eGMS metadata standard. Dublin Core is now an international standard, ISO 15836:2003.

The Dublin Core is currently based on a set of 15 data elements and can be expressed in mark-up languages such as HTML, XML or RDF. The elements and their refinements known as DC-TERMS are listed in Table 3.1.

Table 3.1 Dublin Core elements and refinements (from Dublin Core Metadata Initiative, http://dublincore.org/documents/dcmi-terms)

Data element	Refinement	Description
title		Name given to the resource
	Alternative	
creator		Person or organization responsible for making the content
subject		Topic of the content of the resource
description		An account of the content of the resource
	tableOfContents	
	Abstract	
publisher		Entity responsible for making the resource available
contributor		Person or organization responsible for making contributions to the content
date		Date associated with an event in the lifecycle of the resource
	Created	
	Valid	
	Available	
	Issued	
	Modified	
	dateAccepted	
	dateCopyrighted	
	dateSubmitted	
type		Nature or genre of the content of the resource
format		Physical or digital manifestation of the resource
	Extent	
	Medium	
identifier		Unambiguous reference to the resource such as a URL, a DOI or an ISBN
	bibliographicCitation	
source		Source from which the resource is derived
language		Language of the intellectual content of the resource
relation		Reference to a related resource
	isVersionOf	
	hasVersion	
	isReplacedBy	

Continued on next page

Table 3.1   Continued

Data Element	Refinement	Description
	Replaces isRequiredBy Requires isPartOf hasPart isReferencedBy References isFormatOf hasFormat conformsTo	
coverage		Extent or scope of the content of the resource
	Spatial Temporal	
rights		Information about rights held in and over the resource
	accessRights	

Refinements

Sometimes it is not enough to use a data element on its own. It may need to be qualified in some way to put the data that it contains into some kind of context. For example the DC.date data element in Dublin Core can be refined into: DC.date.Created and DC.date.Modified, in order to distinguish between the date on which a resource was created and the date on which it was modified. Many of the schemas described in the next chapter explicitly allow for refinement of the metadata element, to provide a more specific context for the data. The example below from the British Library's home page shows some actual data expressed as refinements of the DC.date data element:

```
<meta name="DC.date.Created" scheme="W3CDTF"
content="2003-02-03">
<meta name="DC.date.Modified" scheme="W3CDTF"
content="2003-02-03">
```

Each of these examples shows a refinement of the DC.date data element into DC.date.Created and DC.date.Modified. In this particular example the date modified is the same as the date created, i.e. on 3 February 2003.

The National Library of Australia illustrates the principle of refinement with the DC.coverage.spatial data element. It uses the Library of Congress Subject Headings (LCSH) as the source of terms or encoding scheme (defined here as SCHEME=LCSH):

```
<META NAME="DC.Coverage.spatial" SCHEME=''LCSH"
CONTENT="Australia">
```

Refinement of data elements allows organizations considerable flexibility in developing application profiles.

Extensions

Another attribute of metadata schemas is the idea of extensibility. Developers of metadata standards recognize that users may have specific requirements that are not covered by an existing schema. XML allows considerable flexibility in adopting data elements from different schemas and combining them to create a new schema or application profiles suited to the purpose required. The advantage of using elements from existing schemas is that there is greater opportunity for interoperation between applications that have data elements in common. Schemas can also be created without reference to external or pre-existing schemas. An example of an extension is the development of the UK Government's eGMS (UK Office of the e-Envoy, 2003), which is based on Dublin Core but which contains additional data elements or extensions that are specific to eGMS. For example the data element egms.status does not have an equivalent in Dublin Core and can therefore be regarded as an extension of that schema.

Current progress with Dublin Core

The Dublin Core Metadata Initiative is an organization that promotes the 'adoption of interoperable metadata standards'. Its main focus is on improving resource discovery (information retrieval) and on improving cross-domain retrieval on the internet. This has led to the development of interoperable standards and domain-specific applications that are compatible with this (DCMI, 2004).

One way that the DCMI does this is to enable the development of extensions and application profiles to address the needs of different communities of interest. Recent work has focused on the needs of the educational, government and library communities, all of which have developed application profiles for their areas of work. Some of these are described in more detail below.

Government information on the internet – AGLS, GILS and e-GMS

Government information is one of the communities of interest that has developed extensions to Dublin Core to create application profiles for e-government. Government activity on the internet from the mid-1990s led to the early realization that metadata is needed in order to facilitate resource discovery, i.e. to make it easier for the general public to find information on government websites. The US Federal Government, for instance, developed the Government Information Locator Service (GILS), which is designed to help people find information across different federal agencies. It is a decentralized service based on several US federal GILS sites with records mounted by 32 different federal agencies. It is based on the Global Information Locator Service (same acronym) (GILS, n.d.).

The Australian Government Locator Service (AGLS) is a metadata standard for government information on the internet and is based on Dublin Core. It is published in two parts as the AGLS Metadata Element Set (National Archives of Australia, 2002). It consists of 19 data elements with refinements to some of the data elements. The elements are:

- Creator
- Publisher
- Contributor
- Availability*
- Title
- Subject
- Date
- Identifier
- Rights
- Description
- Source
- Language
- Relation
- Coverage
- Function*
- Type
- Format
- Audience*
- Mandate*.

The starred AGLS elements are in addition to the Simple Dublin Core Element Set and are described below:

- *Availability* is primarily intended for use with non-electronic resources and indicates where the resource can be obtained from.
- *Function* relates to the business function of the organization. This is the highest level of a functional analysis of the activities that a government organization undertakes.
- *Audience* is the target audience for the resource. This may be defined in terms of educational level, age range, industry sector or other classification of individuals.
- *Mandate* is an indicator of the legal mandate that requires the resource or service to be provided to the public. This field may refer to specific legislation or provide a URI to the legislation.

The UK government metadata initiative began in 2000 with a review of retrieval of public information from the internet. The Cabinet Office IT Unit (which subsequently became the Office of the e-Envoy) set up a metadata working group which led to the development of the e-Government Metadata Standard (e-GMS), based on Dublin Core. Now in Version 3, e-GMS has 25 data elements. It uses a similar syntax to Dublin Core and can be expressed using XML (a principal requirement for interoperability defined in the e-Government Interoperability Framework (eGIF)). Many of the data elements can be mapped directly on to metadata elements from other standards such as Dublin Core, GILS and AGLS. The standard is dynamic and development is continuing as new demands and applications become apparent.

MARC and libraries

The cultural heritage sector, including museums, libraries and archives, has a long history of using metadata to describe intellectual and artistic works such as books, museum objects and physical records. The sector is now using its long traditions of cataloguing to create metadata for digital resources as well. For example, MARC – the Machine Readable Cataloguing standard – was established in the late 1960s to automate the production of catalogue cards. It was used in early computer-based library catalogues and has evolved into a family of national standards such as USMARC, UKMARC and UNIMARC. In 1999 USMARC (managed by the Library of Congress) and MARC/CAN (managed by the National Library of Canada) were brought under a single standard, MARC21 (Delsey, 2002) which has now been adopted by the British Library and many other cataloguing authorities. The MARC standard forms the basis for shared library cataloguing and for exchange of data between different library management systems. The international standard ISO 2709:1996 defines the record syntax for MARC with the tags and content defined by national cataloguing authorities.

Archives and ISAD

As a result of international collaboration, the International Council on Archives has developed a General International Standard Archival Description, ISAD(G). Its purpose is 'to identify and explain the context and content of archival material in order to promote its accessibility' (International Council on Archives, 2000). It is used for description of archive material and collections. There are 26 data elements defined in the standard. The archival descriptions are based on a model of description with fonds at the highest level, then series and sub-series, then records and finally items. ISAD(G) is designed for use with national standards or as a basis for development of national standards for archives. For instance, the Encoded Archival Description (EAD) standard has cross-walks to and from ISAD(G). EAD is maintained by the Library of Congress and it has a similar role for archives as MARC has for bibliographic records.

Records management applications are based on active management of records using the records lifecycle concept. The international records management standard ISO 15489:2001 defines these concepts. Bodies such as the National Archives in the UK have developed their own application profiles for metadata for use in Electronic Document and Records Management (EDRM) systems. The UK National Archives application profile (Public Record Office, 2002) is based broadly on Dublin Core with extensions for managing processes specifically associated with records such as retention and disposal of records.

ONIX and the publishing industry

The metadata requirements of the publishing sector, in common with those of the library sector, centre on bibliographic data. The sector also has specific rights-handling and e-commerce requirements. The overlap between the two sectors has been a stimulus for a great deal of co-operative activity such as the joint work on ISBNs and the development of the DOI (see p 70). These are both widely used as identification systems and are described in Chapter 4 (pp 68–71).

ONIX (ONline Information eXchange) is a metadata schema used to describe published material (books and serials) and is intended to 'enable publishers to supply "rich" product information to Internet booksellers' (EDItEUR, 2001). It is the result of international collaboration co-ordinated by EDItEUR which represents 90 organizations around the world. Release 2.1 of ONIX issued in 2003 is available as an XML DTD (Document Type Definition) (EDItEUR, 2001). The standard defines over 250 data elements and composite elements that are used to describe book data. These are arranged in 25 product groups, as shown in Table 3.2.

Table 3.2   ONIX product groups

Product group	Name
Group PR1	Record reference number, type and source
Group PR2	Product numbers
Group PR3	Product form
Group PR4	E-publication detail
Group PR5	Series
Group PR6	Set
Group PR7	Title
Group PR8	Authorship
Group PR9	Conference
Group PR10	Edition
Group PR11	Language
Group PR12	Extents and other content
Group PR13	Subject
Group PR14	Audience
Group PR15	Descriptions and other supporting text
Group PR16	Links to image/audio/video files
Group PR17	Prizes
Group PR18	Content items
Group PR19	Publisher
Group PR20	Publishing dates
Group PR21	Territorial rights and other sales restrictions
Group PR22	Dimensions
Group PR23	Related products
Group PR24	Supplier, availability and prices
Group PR25	Sales promotion information

ONIX is designed around a minimum set of data elements so that it is not too arduous for small publishers to adhere to and yet ensures that data is provided in a consistent format that can be exploited by internet booksellers, who in turn can provide information on price, content, etc. to web users (their clients). Major online retailers such as Amazon and Barnes & Noble have taken up ONIX, demonstrating the effectiveness of this approach for exchange of product information. Amazon has identified the following benefits of ONIX:

- Allows publishers to provide single, consistent data set to all customers
- Provides a guideline for all content that can be used for online selling
- ONIX-compliant data supplied directly to Amazon will provide us with a data feed that can be taken as the authoritative source for all fields
- Opportunity for publishers to own how their titles appear on our site.

(Jacobs, 2000)

The following benefits can be added to this list:

- accurate data about publications (because it is originated by the publisher)
- savings in data entry by the retailer.

ONIX is an example of a metadata standard used to facilitate exchange of data between different agents in the supply chain and consequently facilitates e-business.

Multimedia metadata standards

The multimedia sector, represented by the Moving Picture Experts Group, has developed a number of standards for still and moving images. MPEG-7 is an industry metadata standard (ISO/IEC TR 15938-8:2002) that provides a system for describing audiovisual content. The overarching MPEG-21 standard gives the big picture of how data elements relate to one another and has been codified as an international standard ISO/IEC TR 21000. It covers the generation, use, manipulation, management and delivery of multimedia content across different networks and devices.

The Joint Photographic Experts Group has developed standards for digital images. The current standard, JPEG2000 (ISO/IEC 15444-1:2000), is for coding images using an image compression technique based on wavelet technology. The resulting JPX files have metadata elements associated with them, available as an XML schema and as a DTD. The data elements cover details of how the image was created, who was responsible for it and the content of the image.

Education and the IEEE LOM and IMS specifications

With the growth of distance learning and accessibility to resources via the internet there has been increased interest in the retrieval, evaluation and use of digital learning objects. The IEEE LOM (Learning Object

Metadata) standard is intended to enable the management, location and evaluation of learning materials. It applies to digital and non-digital materials such as printed workbooks. It will also facilitate the exchange and sharing of learning objects, via the development of catalogues for instance. The metadata standard describes objects, authors, owners, terms of distribution and format.

The IMS Global Learning Consortium Inc. (www.imsglobal.org/specifications.cfm) has developed a set of data models which define appropriate metadata data elements. Information about the following models is available on the internet:

- IMS Content Packaging (IMS CP) IMS Digital Repositories Specification
- IMS Enterprise Specification
- IMS Learner Information Package (IMS LIP)
- IMS Learning Design Specification
- IMS Question & Test Interoperability (IMS QTI)
- IMS Reusable Definition of Competency or Educational Objective (IMS RDCEO)
- IMS Simple Sequencing Specification.

The Dublin Core Metadata Initiative also has a working group on educational metadata, which is working on extensions to the Dublin Core data elements. There are mappings available between DC-Ed and LOM and IMS CP.

Increasing convergence between sectors and exploitation of a variety of electronic resources means that library and information professionals will need to understand metadata that is applicable to a variety of learning environments such as virtual learning environments. The work of SCRAN (the Scottish Cultural Resources Access Network) is a good example of the way in which a variety of resources in electronic form is being made available to teachers and curriculum development professionals. It is a subscription-based service with learning images available for download from its website. It includes a searchable database of over 300,000 images from museums, galleries and archives. Thumbnail images are available free to non-subscribers and full records with large images, captions, movies and accompanying learning resources are available to subscribers. Its operation depends on metadata to describe the images, their format and availability.

summary

This chapter describes how standards for metadata have developed along differ-ent paths to fit in with the requirements of different communities of interest. A number of data-modelling systems or frameworks have been developed for describing metadata.

The ABC Ontology is a general framework for developing domain-specific descrip-tions and provides a way of describing different ontologies using a common language. The Resource Description Framework (RDF) is a way of modelling and describing metadata and can be expressed in XML or HTML. Its syntax is based on triples: subject, predicate, object, so that, for example, the book 'The Hound of the Baskervilles' (subject) has creator (predicate) 'Arthur Conan Doyle' (object). A third model, the Functional Requirements for Bibliographic Records (FRBR) is more spe-cific, providing a framework for describing products of intellectual and artistic effort, such as books and sound recordings. Indecs, the fourth modelling system described, focuses on the entities and transactions that occur in a commercial publishing envi-ronment. This section finishes with a description of OAIS, an information model for digital archives.

The chapter goes on to look at the role of standards in general terms and to describe specific standards that are used in key domains, starting with Dublin Core. Although widely used for providing access to internet resources, Dublin Core is also seen as an enabler of cross-domain interoperability. This is a general, high-level meta-data standard that has now become an international standard and which forms the basis for many other metadata schemes and application profiles. The MARC stan-dard for libraries has been developing for a long time with the new MARC21 standard being an example of a domain-specific metadata standard. The chapter concludes by looking at the archives community, the publishing industry and mul-timedia standards before describing the range of metadata standards for the learning sector.

References and further sources of information

Consultative Committee for Space Data Systems (2002) *Reference Model for an Open Archival Information System (OAIS)*, CCSDS 650.0-B-1. Blue Book. Issue 1. Washington DC, NASA.

DCMI (2004) *Dublin Core Metadata Initiative Overview*, DCMI, http://dublin-core.org/ [accessed 27/2/2004].

Delsey, T. (2002) *Functional Analysis of the MARC 21 Bibliographic and Hold-ings Formats*, Network Development and MARC Standards Office, Library of Congress, www.loc.gov/marc/marc-functional-analysis/ functional-analysis.html [accessed 12/4/2004].

EDItEUR (2001) *ONIX International: overview and summary list of data ele-ments*, London, Book Industry Communication, and New York, Book Industry Study Group,

www.editeur.org/onixfiles1.2.1/ONIX%20Overview%20R1.2.1.PDF
[accessed 3/2/2004].

Global Information Locator Service, www.gils.net [accessed 28/4/2003].

Gould, S. J. (1989) *Wonderful Life: the Burgess Shale and the nature of history*, New York, W. W. Norton.

IFLA (1998) *Functional Requirements for Bibliographic Records. Final Report*, UBCIM Publications – New Series Vol.19, Munich, K. G. Saur, www.ifla.org/VII/s13/frbr/frbr.pdf [accessed 27/2/2004].

International Council on Archives (2000) *ISAD (G): General International Standard Archival Description: Adopted by the Committee on Descriptive Standards, Stockholm, 19–22 September 1999*, 2nd edn, Ottawa, International Council on Archives.

International DOI Foundation (2003) *The DOI Handbook*, Version 3.3.0, doi:10.1000/182, Oxford, International DOI Foundation, www.doi.org/handbook_2000/glossary.html [accessed 9/4/2004].

International Organization for Standardization (2002) *What Are Standards?* Geneva, International Organization for Standardization, www.iso.ch/iso/en/aboutiso/introduction/index.html [accessed 27/4/2003].

International Organization for Standardization (2003) *Stages for the Development of International Standards*, Geneva, International Organization for Standardization, www.iso.ch.iso.en/stdsdevelopment/whowhenhow/proc/proc.html [accessed 27/4/2003].

ISO 2709:1996. *Information and Documentation – Format for Information Exchange*, Geneva, International Organization for Standardization.

ISO 15489-1:2001. *Information and Documentation – Records Management; Part 1: Gerneral*, Geneva, International Organization for Standardization.

ISO 15836:2003. *Information and Documentation – The Dublin Core Metadata Element Set*, Geneva, International Organization for Standardization.

ISO/IEC 15444-1:2000. *Information Technology – JPEG 2000 Image Coding System – Part I: Core Coding System*, Geneva, International Organization for Standardization.

ISO/IEC TR 15938-8:2002. *Information Technology – Multimedia Content Description Interface – Part 8: Extraction and Use of MPEG-7 Descriptions*, Geneva, International Organization for Standardization.

ISO/IEC TR 21000-1:2001. *Information Technology – Multimedia framework (MPEG-21) – Part 1: Vision, Technologies and Strategy*, Geneva, International Organization for Standardization.

ISO/IEC TR 21000-2:2003. *Information Technology – Multimedia Framework (MPEG-21) – Part 2: Digital Item Declaration*, Geneva, International

Organization for Standardization.

ISO/IEC TR 21000-3:2003. *Information Technology – Multimedia Framework (MPEG-21) – Part 3: Digital Item Identification*, Geneva, International Organization for Standardization.

Jacobs, M. (2000) *ONIX and Amazon.co.uk*, PowerPoint Presentation.

Joint Steering Committee for the Revision of AACR (2002) *Anglo-American Cataloguing Rules*, 2nd edn, 2002 revision, Chicago, IL, American Library Association, Canadian Library Association and CILIP.

Lagoze, C. and Hunter, J. (2001) The ABC Ontology and Model, *Journal of Digital Information*, **2** (2), http://jodi.ecs.soton.ac.uk/Articles/ v02/i02/Lagoze/ [accessed 6/9/2002].

McGuinness, D. L. (2002) Ontologies Come of Age. In Fensel, D. et al. (eds), *Spinning the Semantic Web: bringing the world wide web to its full potential*, Cambridge, MA, MIT Press.

Manola, M. and Miller, E. (eds) (2004) *RDF Primer. W3C Recommendation 10 February 2004*, World Wide Web Consortium, www.w3.org/TR/2004/REC-rdf-primer-20040210/ [accessed 7/3/2004].

National Archives of Australia (2002) *AGLS Metadata Element Set Part 1: Reference Description*, Version 1.3, Canberra, National Archives of Australia, www.naa.gov.au/recordkeeping/gov_online/agls/ metadata_element_set.html [accessed 27/2/2004].

Public Record Office (2002) *Requirements for Electronic Records Management Systems. Part 2: Metadata Standard. 2002 Revision: final version*, Kew, Public Record Office, www.pro.gov.uk/recordsmanagement/ erecords/2002reqs/2002metadatafinal.pdf [accessed 27/2/2004].

Rust, G. and Bide, M. (2000) *The Indecs Metadata Framework: principles, model and data dictionary*, WP1a-006-2.0, Indecs Framework Ltd, www.indecs.org/.

UK Office of the e-Envoy (2004) *E-Government Metadata Standard*, Version 3.0, London, Cabinet Office, http://purl.oclc.org/NET/e-GMS_3 [accessed 24/5/2004].

Walcott, D. (1990) *Omeros*, London, Faber and Faber.

Chapter 4
Purpose i
Resource description

overview

DESCRIPTION IS THE starting point for most metadata schemes and this is therefore the first of the purposes of metadata that is described here. The chapter begins with a discussion of the different characteristics of metadata. It then considers the different aspects of resource description and how it is used to distinguish between different resources. 'Description' underpins other purposes such as retrieval and rights management. Some widely used standards for identifiers such as ISBNs, DOIs, ISSNs, ISTCs and ISANs are described. They are seen as an important part of the successful description of resources. The chapter then expands on other aspects of description by considering in turn data elements for title, creator, bibliographic citation, date, format and description.

Describing resources

The five-point model of the purposes of metadata introduced in Chapter 1 started with resource description, which is the most fundamental of all metadata purposes. It has its origins in the emergence of library catalogues and at its most basic is a way of identifying works. Adequate description is an essential prerequisite for resource discovery (the subject of the next chapter). It also underpins the other applications of metadata. Without a way of identifying and describing a resource, it is impossible to use the associated metadata for other purposes.

For example, in a web search (known generically as resource discovery or information retrieval), some kind of description is needed for retrieved items in order to evaluate the search results and to have an idea of whether the retrieved item fits the requirement. Another example would be in a library. A search of a library catalogue that only yielded accession numbers would not be useful for most searchers. Descriptive data such as the title, author or the format of the item would normally be needed in order to evaluate the items and to make a decision about their relevance and therefore whether to order, borrow, reserve or consult them.

A single data element may not be sufficient to distinguish between items. A search for the author 'Maya Angelou', for instance, would probably bring up several works. In order to select the appropriate item, a wider description than just the name of the author would be needed to assess its relevance. The book title *I Know Why the Caged Bird Sings* may then provide the additional descriptive information that helps a reader to evaluate the retrieved item for relevance and enables that person to distinguish between it and other books by the same author such as *Gather Together in my Name* and *The Heart of a Woman*.

It may not always be clear how complete a description is needed in a given situation. One extreme would be to use the entire item as the description. For instance the entire text of a book could be used to describe the contents of the book. In effect this is what happens with web pages or repositories of electronic journals or e-books. The entire text is available for searching. However, even this may not be complete, because it will not include metadata elements that describe its context or what has happened to it during its life. It also may not include external, independent descriptions of the item, which may themselves be useful sources of data about the book, such as a critical review, or a third-party abstract in a bibliographic database. The biggest drawback of the complete text is its length – often making it impractical as a source of information for rapid evaluation.

Characteristics of metadata elements

There are many different systems for describing resources and they can be grouped together according to the type of resource being described. They vary in complexity from the 15 data elements of the Dublin Core through to the very detailed descriptions allowed for in the MARC 21 standard. Not all the data elements describe the intrinsic qualities of the information resource. This chapter concentrates on those that do and looks at how they handle resource description. The actual data elements used will depend on the resources being described which include bibliographic items (electronic and printed), music, images, text, archives and virtual learning materials.

Metadata characteristics can help to distinguish between different types of metadata and therefore how it should be managed. However, a more useful distinction can be made between intrinsic and applied metadata. Intrinsic metadata is about qualities of the resource itself such as its title, the author and content description. Applied metadata may be contextual, describing how the item described relates to other items or changing attributes such as ownership. The metadata may be about the intended use of the resource. An example is the PICS encoding of the 'Audience' metadata element used in Dublin Core to show that a resource is intended for use by particular age groups, or is designed to exclude specific groups. This allows for parental controls to be implemented, limiting access by children only to approved websites on the internet, for instance. Similarly a record of transactions provides another kind of contextual information which could have a bearing on the provenance of a resource.

This is most usefully described in the IFLA FRBR report (1998) which describes intrinsic attributes of entities in the following terms:

> Attributes, as they are defined in the model, generally fall into two broad categories. There are, on the one hand, attributes that are inherent in an entity, and on the other, those that are externally imputed. The first category includes not only physical characteristics (e.g., the physical medium and dimensions of an object) but also features that might be characterized as labelling information (e.g., statements appearing on the title page, cover, or container). The second category includes assigned identifiers for an entity (e.g., a thematic catalogue number for a musical composition), and contextual information (e.g., the political context in which a work was conceived). Attributes inherent in an entity can usually be determined by examining the entity itself; those that are imputed often require reference to an external source. (IFLA, 1998)

The following metadata elements (mostly derived from Dublin Core, with the exception of bibliographic citation) are described in terms of their relevance to the description purpose. They also play other roles such as retrieval, which is dealt with elsewhere. Dublin Core elements were chosen as the basis for discussion in this chapter, because of its general nature, widespread use and relative familiarity. It has been widely used as the basis for application profiles relevant to specific communities of interest.

These examples are intended to demonstrate the principle of descriptive metadata. The elements are:

- Identifier
- Title
- Creator
- Bibliographic citation
- Date
- Format
- Description.

Identifier

A fundamental part of any description will be some kind of system for uniquely identifying an item. For a small number of items, this could be quite simple, such as the title of a book or piece of music. However with even quite modest collections ambiguity becomes a significant issue, as when two different books share the same title. Identifiers such as ISBNs can be used to distinguish between them. It may also be necessary to distinguish between several copies of a title in a lending library or between individual items of stock in a publisher's warehouse. An identification system can be used for this as well. In both instances the identifier needs to be unique at some level (title, edition, or item, for instance) and unambiguous.

It is important to understand what is being identified. The FRBR model for bibliographic items allows for different levels of granularity of information resource based on a multi-layer model comprising:

Works – e.g. *Harry Potter and the Chamber of Secrets* by J. K. Rowling

Expressions – e.g.
the book
the film directed by Chris Columbus and starring Daniel Radcliffe
the recording read by Stephen Fry

Manifestations – e.g. hardback edition, 2002 (originally published 1998)

Items – such as a particular copy of the book in a public library

An identifier could be applied at any of these levels. An ISBN would, for instance, refer to a manifestation as would a Digital Object Identifier (DOI). However, a catalogue accession number would apply to an individual item as would an item stock number in a bookshop or on an e-commerce system.

DOIs demonstrate the difference between intrinsic metadata and properties associated with an item. Commonly, URLs (universal resource locators) are used to identify web pages – they are used throughout this book, for instance, to provide a reference trail for those seeking further information or background about specific topics. However, URLs describe the location of an electronic resource on the internet. In most cases this happens to coincide with the actual resource and so is effectively used as though it were a resource identifier. But websites change and the content at a particular address may disappear or be replaced. This is one reason that many URL references also give the date that the resource was downloaded or accessed. In other words URLs are not necessarily persistent – they can (and often do) change with time. A DOI on the other hand identifies the object itself (it is primarily intended for digital objects). It is sufficiently flexible to incorporate other identifying elements such as URLs and ISBNs.

URNs or Uniform Resource Names get over the problem of persistence by being attached to the resource itself, rather than its location on the internet, for instance. DOIs are examples of URNs

The idea of name authorities has been carried forward in the Indecs initiative with the concept of 'parties', who may be individuals or organizations. The parties play different roles and can be owners of copyright, creators, customers or performers, for instance. The InterParty project (InterParty, n.d.) is building a network of information that will allow identification of parties across different sectors. This will, for example, help to distinguish between different parties who share the same name, as well as identifying instances where different names are applied to the same party. This is seen as one of the keys to successful interoperability as it allows different agencies to identify parties unambiguously. It will take the form of a Directory of Parties.

International Standard Book Number

The International Standard Book Number or ISBN (ISO 2108:1992) was originally introduced in 1970 and provides a way of uniquely identifying monographs and other non-serial publications. A different ISBN is allocated to each manifestation of a title, so for instance the paperback version of a hardback book will have its own ISBN and a parallel publication on CD-ROM will have a unique and distinct ISBN. The system currently operates as a ten-digit number made up of four elements: place, publisher, book and a check digit at the end.

The ISBN standard is being reviewed and a proposed new standard will take effect from 2007. The new ISBN will consist of a 13-digit code with the following elements:

- *EAN.UCC prefix* (three-digit number allocated by EAN International).
- *Registration group* element, which identifies the national, geographic, language or other grouping within which the ISBN agency allocating the number operates. It is variable in length.
- *Registrant* element which indicates the publisher and varies in length according to the projected output of the publisher.
- *Publication* element allocated by the publisher for the publication. The length of this element will depend on the length of the registrant element and the registration group that precedes it.
- *Check digit* – this is calculated on a modulus 10 algorithm and provides a simple way of checking the validity of a number, helping to identify transcription errors, etc.

In order to manage the allocation of ISBNs, publishers are required to submit ISBN metadata, including the following:

- ISBN
- Product form
- Title
- Contributor
- Edition
- Language
- Imprint
- Publisher
- Country of publication
- Publication date
- ISBN of parent publication (where applicable).

This represents a minimum set of identifying metadata associated with the ISBN.

Digital Object Identifier

The Digital Object Identifier (DOI) is used for identifying intellectual content in a digital environment, including electronic information. It 'provides a framework for managing intellectual content, for linking customers with content suppliers, for facilitating e-commerce, and enabling automated copyright management for all types of media' (International DOI Foundation, 2003). It is intended to form the basis for e-commerce and is co-ordinated by the International DOI Foundation via a network of national agencies.

All DOIs start with the prefix 10, from the Handle System (Corporation for National Research Initiatives, 2003), followed by an alphanumeric (letters and digits) of any length to identify the registrant organization. A forward slash separates the prefix and the suffix, which is assigned to the entity or digital object itself. The suffix may incorporate existing identifiers such as ISBNs. Once assigned, a DOI is persistent – in other words it does not change, even if the ownership changes.

The DOIs are based on three components: resolution, metadata and policy. A DOI can be resolved into associated values such as URLs, other DOIs and other metadata. For instance a digital object with a DOI may have an associated URL which is an internet location that is not usually persistent. The entity associated with the DOI can be moved to another internet location or URL without the need to change the DOI. The DOI can be resolved into multiple values as we see in the following example:

DOI: 10.1004/123456
URL: http://www.pub.com.
URL: http://www.pub2.com/
DLS: loc/repository
XYZ: 1001110011110

Here the DOI value resolves into four sets of associated data.

The metadata associated with a DOI provides the data needed to manage the entity. DOI uses the Indecs principles to analyse the entity and includes a minimum set or 'Kernel' of data common to all DOIs. An entity may have additional metadata from the application profile that it is associated with. For instance a DOI for a publication might use the ONIX application profile.

All terms used in the Kernel and other metadata declarations for DOI Application Profiles should be registered in the Indecs Data Dictionary (iDD). As well as the Kernel metadata, an extended set of metadata can be declared using the DOI Record Metadata Declaration (RMD). The final component is the policy which governs DOI use and is agreed by members of the DOI Foundation.

International Standard Serial Number

ISSNs – International Standard Serial Numbers (ISO 3297:1998) – are administered nationally and co-ordinated by the International Serial Number Organization in Paris. They consist of an eight-digit number, the first seven digits being the unique number allocated to each registered serial title and the last being a check digit. The presentation as two groups of four digits separated by a hyphen is intended to prevent confusion with other international standard numbers such as ISBNs. Over one million ISSNs have been issued. The ISSN standard is likely to be reviewed at some time in the future to allow expansion.

International Standard Text Code

The International Standard Text Code (ISTC) was a draft international standard (ISO/TC46/SC9, 2004) at the time of writing. It has been developed for voluntary allocation of codes to text works independently of their manifestations or expressions (such as books or web pages). The ISTC consists of 16 hexadecimal digits in four groups as follows:

- the issuing agency code, three digits
- the year, four digits
- the unique number, eight digits
- a check digit.

The registering agency will collect the following minimum metadata associated with each text work: title, the name of the author or contributor, a unique identifier for the name of the registrant of the ISTC, and the date of registration.

International Standard Audiovisual Number

ISAN – the International Standard Audiovisual Number (ISO 15706:2002) – is a voluntary system intended for use by the audiovisual industry to uniquely identify any 'work consisting of a sequence of related images, with or without accompanying sound, which is intended to be made visible as a moving image through the use of devices, regardless of the medium of initial or subsequent fixation' (ISO 15706 2002). The ISAN consists of 16 hexadecimal digits, the first 12 of which are unique to each audiovisual work and the remaining four being reserved for part numbers. Human-readable versions of the number have a check digit added. The ISAN is applied to a work and all its manifestations in different media, unlike ISSNs which are unique to each form of a serial. A proposed development is V-ISAN which will incorporate information about the version of the audiovisual work.

Radio-Frequency Identity (RFIDs) tags and identification

In contrast to ISBNs and the other identifiers discussed, Radio-Frequency Identity tags (RFIDs) can be used to identify individual items. RFIDs are becoming widespread in the retail industry and have the potential to be applied to individual retail items, components of those items, or at a macro level to pallets of those items, as part of a logistics system. RFIDs offer an interesting possibility of individually numbering each item independently – providing opportunities for sophisticated management and transaction processing.

RFID tags were invented in 1948, based on the idea that they could be attached to goods and materials and used for identifying and tracking individual items (Landt, 2001). Recent developments include the creation of standards for RFIDs and deployment of the technology in various sectors and application areas such as retail, logistics, vehicle toll systems, ski lift systems and libraries. An RIFD can, for instance, be incorporated into a pallet of goods leaving a factory and then be used to track the pallet in a logistics system. They can be attached to individual goods such as books or CDs and become the basis of a stock control system in a retail outlet.

As RFIDs develop so their data-holding capacity has increased and it is now possible to include significant amounts of data about the object to which the RFID is attached. Where the object represents an information resource, the data on the RFID is effectively metadata. Some libraries have started to use RFIDs to track individual books and this technology could eventually replace barcodes. RFIDs can also be used for tagging CDs as part of retail security and stock control systems. As the cost of individual RFID tags continues to fall and the technology develops, the pressure will be on for large retailers, wholesalers and manufacturers to adopt the technology in order to make efficiency gains.

RFIDs have generated some controversy, which has been widely reported in the press (Schofield, 2003), with arguments against use of the technology ranging from religious grounds to loss of privacy.

Title

Although titles are extensively used to identify resources, they are not always descriptive of the content. In web pages the title is probably the most widely used metadata element and in HTML is delimited by the tags <title> and </title>. This mark-up is frequently used by search engines and by browsers to establish what is displayed at the top of the web page. The actual text of the page may in fact differ from the text within the title tags.

Book titles show considerable variation depending on whether it is the full title, a common representation of the title, or a particular translation of the original title. All these titles will cause confusion in the identification of an information resource unless there is some way to distinguish between them. Consistent cataloguing rules, for instance AACR2 and ISBD(ER), provide rules on sources of information. They can be used to establish which version of the title takes priority, or even how to deal with different title origins. Cataloguers have to deal with questions such as: does the title of a series of monographs appear before or after the title of the individual monograph? They also have to deal with subtitles and this may provide additional confusion in the description of an item. For example, Charles Darwin's famous work is often referred to as *Origin of Species*. Yet when it was originally published in 1859, its full title was *On the Origin of Species by Means of Natural Selection, or the Preservation of Favoured Races in the Struggle for Life*. This can cause problems when searching for items in a catalogue and certainly causes confusion when trying to determine which item is relevant to a particular request.

In the discussion about FRBR in Chapter 2, four different levels of entity were identified, each with its own data elements, including title. A work such as *Origin of Species* may be expressed as a written book which is manifest in a number of different editions and reprints. In this case they all share the same title and have to be distinguished by other means such as edition, place of publication and publisher. These will be different expressions of the first edition, which is itself a manifestation of the original work.

Work: On the Origin of Species by Means of Natural Selection
Manifestation: Text of the First Edition
Expression 1: London: J Murray, 1859
Expression 2: New York, NY: D Appleton and company, 1860

Thus it is possible to see the benefits and limitations of title as a means of describing information. In some contexts it may be sufficient to distinguish between different items; in others it will be one of a number of attributes that in combination provide a sufficiently detailed description of the item to assess its relevance or to uniquely identify it.

Creator

Creator covers a wide range of possible relationships and may imply intellectual property rights such as copyright. For printed publications, the author is usually the 'creator' entity. However, it also applies to editors of series of compiled works as well as illustrators and translators.

For web pages the situation can become quite complex. For instance, some organizations do not attribute the content of web pages to named individuals, but to departments or the organization itself, often for the following reasons:

- to protect individuals against harassment – particularly if the content may be viewed as controversial in some quarters
- to indicate corporate responsibility – especially for content written by an individual or group of individuals in an official capacity
- to provide a more reliable point of contact for those who wish to act on the content of the web page – the individual authors may move on, in which case the department may be the more helpful point of contact.

Well established conventions such as the *AACR2 Cataloguing Rules* (Joint Steering Committee for the Revision of AACR, 2002) provide a good guide for expressing author names in publications. The citation rules for many refereed journals also have their own conventions for author names. The rules are not so clearly defined for web pages, and the permissive metadata standards used in this arena such as Dublin Core do not specify how a creator's name is expressed. Within communities of practice there is more insistence on the need for consistency, which has led to the development of cataloguing rules in some contexts such as e-prints and subject gateways. The question arises should it be surname, followed by the initials, or full name, or the title followed by the first name and then the family name? Even in the relatively well defined area of bibliographic records there are variances in author name which can cause problems when it comes to reliable identification of a publication. Different amounts of data may be available for different publications by the same author. In the previous example about *Origin of Species*, the author could be expressed as:

C. Darwin
Charles Darwin
C. R. Darwin
Charles R. Darwin
Charles Robert Darwin
Charles Darwin 1809–1882

And then there are the inversions of the surname and given names: Darwin, C. etc. The last example in the list above introduces the dates of Charles Darwin's lifespan, affording another way of discriminating between this particular individual and other authors who may share the same name. Where transliteration from a different script is concerned, there is an added level of variation. For instance is it Tchaikovsky or Chaikowski? Is it Mao Tse-Tung or Mao Zedong?

A name may not be sufficient to distinguish between different authors. For example the author 'Steve Jones' comes in at least three distinct varieties, which becomes clear when the cataloguing data reveals their dates of birth. There is Steve Jones (b. 1944), the biologist who wrote *The Language of the Genes: biology, history and the evolutionary future*. There is Steve Jones (b. 1953), the sports writer and author of *Endless Winter: the inside story of the rugby revolution*, and there is Steve Jones (b. 1961), the music critic and author of *Rock Formation: music, technology and mass communication*. Authority lists which include additional data such as the date of birth provide an added level of specificity and makes identification of items (such as books) more reliable.

Where the creator is an organization the issue of name change may arise. Official bodies may be subject to reorganization and this can affect the publication record of a revised text. For example, the Office of the e-Envoy, responsible in the UK for enabling the establishment of e-government initiatives, was created in 1999 from the Cabinet Office IT Unit (CITU). A more radical change took place with the transformation of the UK government's Ministry of Agriculture, Fisheries and Food (MAFF) to DEFRA (Department for the Environment, Food and Rural Affairs) in 2001. This can lead to problems identifying items reliably or in describing them accurately when they have been identified. Cataloguers deal with items 'in hand', so that the publication details reflect the situation at the point of publication. This breaks the connection between items that would otherwise be seen as part of the same group. Bodies such as the National Archives deal with this by the use of authority lists that make those connections

Name authorities

For many years libraries have developed name authorities, following AACR2 (Joint Steering Committee for the Revision of AACR, 2002) for instance. Archivists have also developed a system for a name authority, ISAAR (CPF) for Corporate Bodies, Persons and Families (International Council on Archives, 1996) which is used in several countries. Name authorities ensure the consistency of catalogues and help to eliminate ambiguity, one of the reasons for identifications systems.

Bibliographic citation

Following the MARC standard (Library of Congress, 2003) or the IFLA FRBR model (IFLA, 1998), the citation details are an important part of the description of the information container. The bibliographic citation includes elements already discussed, such as title and creator. However, it also includes other distinguishing details such as publisher, place of publication and date of publication. Different types of bibliographic records such as those for journal articles will also include details of the journal and the relevant volume and issue numbers. Conventions for citations such as AACR2 or the multiplicity of conventions used by refereed journals provide rules for the order and format of the citation details. The intention of the citation details is to uniquely identify and help in the location of the resource being described. Again there must be a consideration of consistency in citation conventions. Some applications such as the Endnote bibliographic management tool keep generic records and output records in different formats according to the requirements of the publisher. Even then these conventions may be limited to the order in which items are cited and the punctuation that separates the different data elements. This means that cataloguers have to refer to standard cataloguing rules for information on how to cite the elements correctly.

Date

Date information occurs in a number of contexts. It may be an intrinsic property of an information resource – for example date of creation, date of publication, date of revision. It may also be an externally imposed data element that has more to do with the management of the resource, for example web page revision or expiry dates, or review dates for electronic records. Date information can also refer to when something was done to the resource – such as date of disposal, date of change of ownership. This type of date information is not intrinsic to the resource or information container and would not normally be considered to be resource description. However, the date of creation or modification probably is intrinsic and can also be used as part of the identification and description of an item.

Format

Format information is particularly important for electronic information resources and may provide the key to future access to the resource. It is evident in digital images, many of which are created with a great deal of proprietary metadata about the format, the application and version used to create or modify the image, the storage format; and the medium used to store the data. This descriptive information becomes important when it comes to reconstructing information by means of migration or by emulating the original applications.

Format does not only apply to electronic resources. The format of a printed work may also be relevant and may refer to whether a book is hardcover or paperback, and the physical size of the document, and whether or not it contains illustrations. This type of information is particularly helpful for managing resources. Do the books fit on a standard shelf, for instance, or do they have to be kept with the outsize material with special shelving capable of accommodating this material? The format information that describes the resource will help a manager to decide how it should be handled.

Description

On the face of it the 'Description' data element (in Dublin Core) is most directly relevant to the purpose of resource description discussed in this chapter. However, descriptive information may not be an intrinsic property of the information resource. An author's abstract in a journal article or an introduction from a monograph is intrinsic, but an externally produced abstract or summary is not intrinsic, it is applied to the resource. This is particularly the case for the description of physical objects or images.

There are different approaches to resource description. For example, an external abstract may be enriched with controlled terms to enhance retrieval. Alternatively it may be purely free text: the most likely outcome of using authors' abstracts or publishers' promotional material. The description will depend on the purpose of the abstract and this will inform the approach that should be adopted. Many secondary sources specialize in preparing abstracts on indexed items. The same article may have quite different abstracts which are geared to different audiences. The questions to ask are:

- Does it help users to assess the relevance of a retrieved item?
- Does it enhance retrieval – for instance by use of enriching controlled terms?
- Is it intended to sell the item – as in publishers' promotional material?
- Can it be used to evaluate a resource – is this an independent expert's commentary or review of the item?

The description data element can therefore be applied to this purpose even though it is not necessarily intrinsic to the resource itself.

summary

The data elements used to illustrate the descriptive purpose of metadata area are designed for other purposes such as information retrieval, interoperability and rights management. The level of description required will depend on the context. For instance, a title may be sufficient for a library user to distinguish between different books by an author. A fuller description may be needed if several titles from an Amazon online bookshop were being evaluated to inform a purchase decision. In practice several data elements would probably be used to make an evaluation. Identifiers are a particularly complex area, there being a variety of different identification systems that can be applied. For instance, an electronic resource may have a DOI, an URL and a URI. Other descriptive elements such as title may be applied at a number of levels (using the FRBR model) – the Work, the Manifestation, the Expression or the Item. Throughout the discussion on descriptive metadata elements, the theme of consistency has recurred. The adoption of consistent cataloguing rules is one way of helping to uniquely identify items and forms the basis for the development of authority lists. In the library and archive fields there has been considerable progress in the development of name authority lists that can be used to distinguish between similar sounding items and to consolidate variations around a party name (such as an author) or information resource (such as an archive or book) for consistent retrieval.

References and further sources of information

Corporation for National Research Initiatives (2003) *Handle System*, CNRI, www.handle.net/introduction.html [accessed 5/5/2003].

International Council on Archives (1996) *ISAAR (CPF): International Standard Archival Authority Record for Corporate Bodies, Persons and Families*, final ICA approved version, Paris, International Council on Archives, www.ica.org/biblio/isaar_eng.pdf [accessed 28/2/2004].

International DOI Foundation (2003) *The DOI Handbook*, Version 3.3.0, doi:10.1000/182, Oxford, International DOI Foundation, www.doi.org/hb.html [accessed 4/2/2004].

International Federation of Library Associations (1998) *Report on the IFLA Functional Requirements for Bibliographic Records*, Munich, K. G. Saur.

InterParty, www.interparty.org/ [accessed 2/5/2003].

ISO 2108:1992. *Information and Documentation – International Standard Book Numbering (ISBN)*, Geneva, International Organization for Standardization.

ISO 3297:1998. *Information and Documentation – International Standard Serial Number (ISSN)*, Geneva, International Organization for Standardization.

ISO 15706:2002. *Information and Documentation – International Standard Audiovisual Number (ISAN)*, Geneva, International Organization for Standardization.

ISO/TC46/SC9 (2004) *International Standard Text Code (ISTC)*, ISO Committee Draft 21047, International Organization for Standardization, www.nc.-bcn.ca/tc46sc9/21047.htm [accessed 5/02/2004].

Joint Steering Committee for the Revision of AACR (2002) *Anglo-American Cataloguing Rules*, 2nd edn, 2002 revision, Chicago, IL, American Library Association, Ottawa, Canadian Library Association, and London, CILIP. Amendments published annually.

Landt, J. (2001) *Shrouds of Time: the history of RFID*, AIM Inc., www.aimglobal.org.

Library of Congress (2003) *MARC 21. Concise format for bibliographic data*, concise edn, Washington DC, Library of Congress, http://lcweb.loc.gov/marc/bibliographic [accessed 5/2/2004].

Schofield, J. (2003) Tracked and Tested, *Guardian*, (19 June), www.guardian.co.uk/online/story/0,3605,979990.00.html [accessed 13/7/2003].

Chapter 5
Purpose ii
Information retrieval

overview

METADATA STANDARDS SUCH as Dublin Core and e-GMS are primarily focused on improving retrieval of web resources. This chapter considers the role of metadata in information retrieval. It begins with a review of information retrieval concepts and measures of retrieval performance before considering ways in which metadata can improve retrieval. Reference is made to models for resource description and subject indexing. This includes an examination of the role of indexing, the development of encoding schemes, and use of controlled terms from thesauri, taxonomies and classification schemes. These can all contribute to delivery of an efficient information retrieval system. This is illustrated with examples of portals, subject gateways and intranets. The final part of the chapter examines the relationship between subject indexing and computational methods of retrieval. The chapter concludes with a discussion of alternatives to metadata and the relative merits of the different emergent approaches to resource discovery.

Information retrieval concepts

In order to put metadata into context, a brief discussion of information retrieval is necessary. The history of information retrieval theory in the 20th century is reflected in the development of many specialist search engines and database systems. For very large document collections, ranking of search results is critical to the utility of the search system and this has shifted the emphasis of retrieval systems away from simple text retrieval towards statistical approaches.

Boolean logic

Set theory has developed considerably since George Boole, a 19th-century mathematician, invented Boolean algebra from which logical operators for combining sets arose. These basic operators are available on most information retrieval systems today and are a fundamental part of searching the internet and metadata collections such as library catalogues. The commonly used operators are:

- AND – retrieves documents containing both search terms or expressions linked by the 'AND' operator
- OR – retrieves documents containing either search term or expression linked by the 'OR' operator
- NOT – retrieves documents containing the first search term but not the second search term linked by the 'NOT' operator.

In the example illustrated in Figure 5.1, a library catalogue contains details on books about pets. In the first example an enquirer wants books about both cats and dogs. The area of overlap between the two circles represents the set of books on 'Cat AND Dog'. Another reader might be less discriminating and may want anything on either cats or dogs. This is represented by the total area of both circles 'Cat OR Dog'. In the third example, someone may be looking for books that are exclusively about cats and which do not mention dogs at all: 'Cat NOT Dog'. This is represented by the left-hand circle, but excluding that part which overlaps with the circle for 'Dog'. Although this type of search facility is available on most commonly used search engines on the internet, most users do not explicitly use Boolean operators. They tend to be limited to advanced searchers.

Figure 5.1

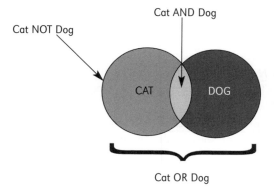

Boolean operators

Google and other search systems use the 'AND' operator implicitly to link two or more search terms that are entered without operators between them.

Precision and recall

The main focus in this chapter is on subject retrieval. In the context of the internet, retrieval can be problematic. There are two different issues:

- Lack of precision – internet searches often result in the retrieval of too much material, most of it irrelevant.
- Low recall – relevant material is missing because the search is not comprehensive enough or the resource is 'hidden' in the deep web.

These two requirements of precision and recall are complementary, in that recall is often improved at the expense of precision and vice versa. For instance a search on the *Washington Post* during two weeks in November 2003 for articles about Hillary Clinton could be done to maximize recall. A query using the term 'Clinton' yielded 118 matches. This is not very precise because it includes references to President Bill Clinton or to Senator Hillary Rodham Clinton or to both. A more specific query using the term 'Hillary Rodham Clinton' yielded 10 matches which were all relevant. However, it left out at least four relevant items that were retrieved during the more general search, so precision has improved at the expense of recall. The ideal outcome would be to find everything that was published on Hillary Clinton in the *Washington Post* during the two week period (good recall), but only those that specifically mentioned her name (good precision). Precision and recall are two widely used measures of retrieval performance.

Precision = $\dfrac{\text{No. of relevant documents retrieved}}{\text{Total no. of documents retrieved}}$

Recall = $\dfrac{\text{No. of relevant documents retrieved}}{\text{Total no. of relevant documents}}$

These two measures can be expressed in terms of the following contingency table (Table 5.1).

Table 5.1 Contingency table for information retrieval

	Relevant	Non-relevant	
Retrieved	$A \cap B$	$\bar{A} \cap B$	B
Not retrieved	$A \cap \bar{B}$	$\bar{A} \cap \bar{B}$	$\bar{B}$
	A	$\bar{A}$	N

$$precision = \frac{A \cap B}{B}$$

$$recall = \frac{A \cap B}{A}$$

The contingency table in Table 5.1 can be used to show the relationship between precision and recall. B is the set of items retrieved, $\bar{B}$ is the remainder and together they add up to the total number of items, N. Similarly, A is the set of items that is relevant to a query, $\bar{A}$ is the remainder (i.e. items not relevant to the query) and together they add up to the total number of items, N. The expression $A \cap B$ is the overlap between the set of relevant items, A, and retrieved items, B.

Precision and recall are widely used for evaluating the effectiveness of retrieval systems. In practice they are difficult to measure, especially in a dynamic and diverse environment such as the internet, because it is necessary to know the total population of relevant items on the system. It can also be difficult to assess the relevance of a retrieved item, especially if only one item is actually needed – the others in effect providing duplicate answers.

Also, it is not always possible to predict the effectiveness of a particular search query for retrieving relevant items. If different terminology is used by the searcher and the creator of the text, there is likely to be a mismatch. For instance a technical paper on 'bovine spongiform encephalopathy' might refer throughout to 'BSE' and never use the full term. A search on the full term would then miss this relevant item.

Bayesian Inference and the probabilistic model

The probabilistic model is an application of Bayesian Inference and provides the basis for weighting individual query terms and documents.

Bayesian Inference provides a way of 'calculating the probabilistic relationship between multiple variables and determining the extent to which one variable impacts on another' (Autonomy, n.d.). Term frequency across a document collection provides a statistical method for ranking documents. Where feedback is built into the system (either explicitly where the searcher selects the most relevant items or implicitly by the system monitoring use of retrieved items to assess relevance) the results can be refined by a process of iteration.

Shannon's Information Theory

Shannon's Information Theory, originally published in 1948, underpins digital communications systems today. It looks at the probability that a particular unit of communication (such as a word or phrase) will occur in any given piece of text. The maximum amount of information is conveyed by a unit of information when the probabilities are equal. There is quite a lot of redundancy built into most text-based systems. The less frequently a unit of communication occurs, the more information it conveys. This can be used to compute the incremental value of a two-word term over its separate components. In other words compound terms (or co-location of relevant words) can improve the ranking of a retrieved document. This approach leads to a mathematical analysis that is independent of linguistic analysis.

Retrieval on the internet

Metadata can be used to put search terms into some kind of semantic context – in effect telling the search engine or other application how to deal with a particular metadata element. This is typically seen in a library catalogue where it is possible to distinguish between the author 'Green' (i.e. the name of a person) and the keyword 'green' which describes a topic such as the colour green. This kind of semantic distinction is becoming available on the internet, using Dublin Core metadata elements (or the equivalent) embedded in web pages. An example of this emerging practice is the Directgov website (www.direct.gov.uk) which provides a portal to UK government websites.

One way forward is to use metadata to describe the subject content of a resource and enrich the text of the web page. Where there are alternative expressions used to describe a particular subject, they can be included in the metadata. We saw earlier how a search on 'bovine spongiform encephalopathy' might fail because the most relevant documents referred only to 'BSE'. This could be overcome by adding the term 'bovine spongiform encephalopathy' to the metadata. This would then be made available as a retrieval term by the search software.

Some web authors include the variant words or synonyms in the text of their documents. This provides an alternative to explicit metadata elements for subject content. However, this depends on the consistency with which authors apply synonyms to the document and how comprehensively they do it. A more consistent approach is to use controlled terms selected from a thesaurus and to allow the search engine to make the connection between the controlled term and its synonyms automatically, by means of synonym rings (see p 88).

Search engines and ranking

Search engines are evolving and their approach to retrieval on the internet has changed. The precise algorithms used by search engines tend not to be published, because of the potential this gives web creators to manipulate search outcomes. However, it is possible to see a pattern in the way in which they have developed between the mid-1990s and the early 2000s.

At the simplest level a search engine can simply look for all occurrences of a word or a phrase in its database of internet resources. It may list the retrieved items in the order in which it found the items. At a slightly more sophisticated level it could list retrieved items in chronological or in reverse chronological order. This is manageable if a few items are retrieved, but not particularly helpful for internet searches which can result in thousands or even millions of hits. Given the general reluctance to use more than one search term or to refine search strategies, some kind of relevance ranking becomes essential.

The first thing internet search engines started to do to overcome this was to develop ranking algorithms based on the number of occurrences of a search term in the web page retrieved. Although this can be helpful, it tends to favour longer documents where there is a greater chance of the search term occurring multiple times. The next refinement was to look at the frequency of occurrence of a search term. For instance, five occurrences of a search term in a document 500 words long (a frequency of 1 in 100) gives a higher frequency of occurrence than, say, ten occurrences of the same search term in a web resource which is 10,000 words long (a frequency of 1 in 1,000).

The big breakthrough was to realize that the position of a word, its context, will have a bearing on its relevance. Users of Library catalogues will be familiar with the differences that occur when searching for a word in the title, or in the text of a summary or abstract. A similar principle can be applied to websites. If the word is in the title of a web page, search engines now tend to attribute greater weight to it than if it only occurs in the main body of the page. Matches to the title words push the resource up the ranking of hits.

Metadata can now play a role in putting a term into context. Unfortunately this is a feature that was exploited unscrupulously by a minority of web authors who embedded repetitions of keywords in the metadata. This manipulation was carried to its logical conclusion by putting in the name of competitors in the metadata fields of their home pages. This meant that searches for a competitor's name would retrieve the site indexed in this way – a good way of alerting competitors' customers to the existence of your products or services. Because of the possibility of overt manipulation, most search engines now reduce the weight attached to metadata terms and some ignore them altogether.

There is a rebound of interest in metadata for retrieval, however, as portals which allow access to limited domains are realizing the benefits of metadata exploitation for retrieval. For instance, UKOnline – an experimental portal for official government sites (now replaced by Direct-gov) – allows users the choice of searching on keywords that have been assigned to individual pages. For example a search for 'Pensions' on UKOnline in November 2003 retrieved 101,777 items. A more precise search, using the Advanced Search feature to search for 'Pensions' in the keyword field, yielded 5,937 items. Although there is considerable overlap between the two sets of retrieved items, the first search yielded items that happened to mention pensions as part of the benefits offered to prospective employees and other incidental mentions. Where a conscious decision was made by the author to index the item with 'Pensions' in the keyword metadata field, the items were more likely to be relevant.

Commentators in the search engine field have suggested that metadata elements have very limited use for general internet search engines and it was probably never a realistic expectation in any case that they would help. Most search engines ignore even the most common metadata elements from widely accepted standards such as Dublin Core (Sullivan, 2002a, 2002b; Goodman, 2002a, 2002b). Sullivan and Goodman both concede that metadata is useful for on-site search engines – where the search is limited to that site and so there is less problem of overt manipulation or spamming. It is also useful for portals to related information and on intranets – again where there is control over the content and the way that it is used.

Adding metadata to enhance the retrieval of web pages is worthwhile if the resource is directed at a community of interest with a defined approach to subject indexing and retrieval, as was shown in the example above. This is now changing as more sophisticated interfaces and portals are being developed. Where there is a portal to controlled, authenticated and authoritative sites, metadata provides an added level of quality to the retrieval. For example the 'JustAsk!' service operated by the Community Legal Service contains access to legal information from over 300 websites covering England and Wales. All the participants use a common taxonomy to select keywords which are encoded into the relevant web pages. This means that users can navigate to relevant web pages via the classification headings, or can search on the keywords. A search on 'data protection' yielded five sources of information and two sources of online legal advice, with links to the relevant sites.

Spiders, crawlers, robots and ranking

Search engines have to cover enormous volumes of material very rapidly in order to provide reasonably up-to-date access to web resources. A search engine has three components: robots, indexers and sorters. The robots are, as their names imply, automated programs that search for websites, and document them (by making a reference or by taking a copy) and following any links in the site. The robots are sometimes called crawlers or spiders and the action is known as 'crawling' or 'spidering' the web. When a searcher puts in a search query the search engine consults the index that has been constructed by the system. The results are then sorted into a ranked order. Most search engines offer a choice between chronological order and ranking by relevance. The precise algorithms used to determine relevance are usually kept secret to prevent overt manipulation by the authors of web pages.

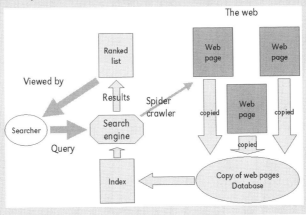

Synonym rings

Many search engines support synonym rings. These can be created from a simplified thesaurus, which associates terms that are synonyms or quasi-synonyms. For instance, the following terms could be associated with one another in a synonym ring:

> personnel managers, human resources managers, industrial relations managers, training managers

Another example of a synonym ring groups together related terms from a thesaurus:

> addiction, alcohol abuse, drug abuse, smoking, substance abuse

In a structured thesaurus, these terms would be related to one another with the following relationships:

> USE
> USE FOR
> RT (related term)
> BT (broader term)
> NT (narrower term).

A search for any one of these terms would retrieve all the terms in the synonym ring. This improves recall at the expense of precision. Precision can be improved by being more selective in the relationships included in the synonym ring – for example by limiting the synonym ring to true synonyms, defined by the USE and USE FOR relationships. An alternative approach is to be more inclusive (by using quasi-synonyms, defined by RT, BT and NT relationships, as well as USE and USE FOR), but to generate drop-down lists in response to queries and allowing users to explicitly selected related terms.

Subject indexing and retrieval

The concepts of subject indexing can be applied to internet portals and gateways and to intranets to enhance retrieval performance. Some of the data elements used for resource description, such as 'title', 'description' and 'creator', are also used for information retrieval. Retrieval performance can be improved by use of controlled terminology to describe the subject content of the resource. Classification of material according to a taxonomy can also provide a precise route in to relevant material.

Thesauri and taxonomies

There are a number of steps that can be taken to enhance the quality of retrieval of web resources:

- If the organization has invested effort in defining a standard vocabulary or terminology, it is possible to enrich web pages with the 'preferred' terms from the thesaurus, and to configure the search engine to look for the appropriate metadata.
- This process can be automated so that web pages are processed to identify potential indexing terms. The preferred term is attached as metadata when a recognized synonym is found in the text of the document. This ensures that a consistent term is used to describe a concept regardless of the actual words used on the web page. This approach can be enhanced by providing users with a drop-down list or a navigable hierarchy to find suitable 'preferred' search terms.
- A taxonomy can be used to classify and organize material on the site. The taxonomy may be applied manually or automatically based on recognition of keywords in the text. The user then has access to the resources by means of a map or drop-down lists of categories under which the web pages fall. This kind of approach supports polyhierarchy in that it is possible to apply more than one category to a web page, allowing different users to access the same resource by different routes.

Thesaurus relationships

Thesaurus relationships are defined in ISO 2788:1986 and an excellent and detailed description of them is given in Aitchison, Gilchrist and Bawden (2000). A term may be associated with other terms, defined by relationships. If we take 'Bacteria' as our lead-in term (Haynes, Huckle and Elliot, 2002) the following relationships can be defined:

Bacteria
   BT: Microorganisms
   BT: Pathogens
   NT: E coli
   NT: Legionella
   NT: Listeria
   NT: Salmonella

BT stands for broader term. These are more general terms and are higher up the hierarchy. The thesaurus may have several levels of hierarchy – which can provide a useful navigation tool. In this example Bacteria has two broader terms, 'Micro-organisms' and 'Pathogens'.

NT stands for narrower term. These are more specific terms, lower down the hierarchy. A term may have more than one narrower term. The narrower terms of Bacteria are 'E coli', 'Legionella', 'Listeria' and 'Salmonella'.

The next relationship is illustrated by the example of 'Addiction' from the *HSE Thesaurus* (Haynes, Huckle and Elliot, 2002).

> Addiction
> BT: Psychiatric disorders
> RT: Alcohol abuse
> RT: Drug abuse
> RT: Smoking
> RT: Substance abuse

RT stands for related term. This relationship connects associated concepts. It is a useful way of broadening the search or providing a route to alternative search terms (or indexing terms). This feature can be particularly helpful for generating drop-down lists of alternative search terms. In this example, entering 'Addiction' would produce a drop-down list of alternative search terms including 'Alcohol abuse', 'Drug abuse', 'Smoking' and 'Substance abuse'.

The final relationships, use and use for, are illustrated with the following example:

> Personnel managers
> UF: Human resources managers
> UF: Industrial relations managers
> UF: Training managers
> BT: Functional managers

USE indicates a preferred term. A thesaurus represents a 'controlled vocabulary' to ensure consistency of indexing (and retrieval). The entry for 'Training managers' in the thesaurus would have USE 'Personnel managers' as its entry.

USE FOR indicates a non-preferred term. This points to synonyms of a preferred term. In this example 'Personnel managers' is the preferred term and the UF relationships point to the non-preferred terms that would be synonyms.

A thesaurus is a representation of knowledge, the relationships between terms reflecting assumptions about the nature of a subject or discipline.

The terms 'taxonomy', 'thesaurus' and 'classification' are often used interchangeably. Some distinctions can be made between them, however. A thesaurus is normally made up of terms (word or phrases) which represent single concepts. These terms may be classified for ease of management or arranged alphabetically. Taxonomies and classification systems are ways of organizing or grouping entities, whether they be species of plants or insects, documents, web pages or ideas. Each category may be a complex concept made up of simpler concepts, or it may be a class of objects used for discriminating between objects. A thesaurus on the other hand is usually made up of simple terms which can be put together to construct a more complex description.

In indexing theory there is a distinction made between pre-co-ordinate and post-co-ordinate indexes. A pre-co-ordinate index co-ordinates simpler terms and concepts to produce a category or term that can be used for searching. For example an index in a recipe book may be organized by dishes e.g. 'Carrot cake', which would be a pre-co-ordinated index term. In contrast, a searchable database of recipes may have an index term 'Carrots' and a separate term for 'Cakes'. This is a post-coordinate system, because the terms are put together (or co-ordinated) at the search stage rather than the indexing stage.

Portals and gateways

The role of metadata in information retrieval has been brought to the fore again by the growth of portal technology and extranet features on the internet as well as on intranets. A common theme of these diverse interfaces is the improved control over the range of web resources that are referenced.

A portal is a gateway to a range of electronic sources (usually in the context of the internet). An example is the Directgov website. Within individual sites, the site search engines can be configured to look for terms in the description, subject category and keyword fields. This enables individual web pages to be enriched with metadata made up of standard terms selected from a controlled vocabulary such as a thesaurus. However, the best way of ensuring good retrieval is still to make sure that all significant retrieval terms occur in the visible part of the web pages, either as part of the title or in the first few lines of the text.

Tagged metadata elements such as the Dublin Core subject.keyword data element allow for greater search precision. Use of metadata is a key part of the semantic web and this makes it possible to limit searches to specific fields (or data elements). Naming specific fields puts the search terms into their proper contexts.

Many academic institutions such as universities and colleges have created their own indexes and interfaces to selected internet resources.

Initiatives to co-ordinate these activities across institutions nationally and internationally, have resulted in subject gateways focused on specific areas of academic discipline. They have arisen in response to the need for academic institutions to provide pointers to high-quality resources on the internet and to help students and researchers to filter through the huge volume of material to find reliable and authoritative sources of information.

This approach depends on teams of human indexers who can evaluate and judge the quality of sites that they find and then attribute metadata to those sites. The metadata is stored in databases, which are searched by users to provide a list of links to appropriate web resources. Although it is possible to search individual fields, most users choose not to, preferring simple 'Google'-type boxes. The enriched records created by the indexers provide better recall and greater precision than simply searching the uncontrolled text of the web pages. For example the OMNI gateway (www.omni.ac.uk) provides access to biomedical resources on the internet as part of the Resource Discovery Network (www.rdn.ac.uk). The Renardus initiative (www.renardus.org), funded by the European Commission, provides a cross-searching facility across several European subject gateways covering 64,000 web-based resources. It includes the RDN described above, the Finnish Virtual Library, the Danish Electronic Research Library (deff) and several subject-specialist resources. It is possible to search by text in the title, subject or description fields of the gateway records, by creator or by Dewey Decimal Classification code. The search facilities also allow users to limit results by document type, language or country of publication, based on metadata applied to the resources being searched.

With wider adoption of general metadata standards such as Dublin Core, it ought to be easier for the web gateway providers to harvest relevant data for their databases of web resources, and this is a potential application that may extend the range of the subject-based gateways in the future and possibly reduce the effort (and expense) required to maintain them.

Extranets provide controlled access to website resources for specified communities via the internet. They are normally password protected so that only authorized users such as members of a professional body, staff from a distributed company, customers of a business or commercial partners of an enterprise, for instance, have access. This type of environment is closed and this means that there is much greater scope for the provider to manage the way in which users access and retrieve information. In this type of environment it is possible to provide subject access via a number of routes:

- free text searching
- searching for controlled indexing terms
- searching for terms in a specified field
- searching for terms across several fields.

However, this depends on being able to attribute metadata elements to web resources.

Intranets

Intranets can be more tightly controlled than a group of websites, or the internet. Yet all too often intranets grow in an uncontrolled manner and do not have a coherent structure. It is common for each department within an organization to have considerable autonomy about what goes on the intranet and the result can be more like a scaled-down version of the internet than a structured information resource. Content management systems can help organizations to manage their intranets and websites more effectively. However, even with use of the additional metadata elements to describe the content of a particular page or site, there may be an issue of consistency. The indexing of resources is expensive in terms of human effort, and lack of suitably skilled staff can be a limiting factor. This absence can affect the quality and consistency of indexing. Web managers need to be aware of these issues when they are implementing a metadata strategy.

Using data elements to refine search results

Data elements provide a context for search results. One of the features of metadata is that individual fields are labelled. This allows some search engines and search interfaces to provide a 'search by form' or 'query by example' approach. In Figure 5.2, entering a term into the appropriate field makes it possible to retrieve relevant items. This kind of approach is seen in tightly managed systems where the contents of the information repository can be controlled and structured with embedded data elements or are linked to separate metadata records.

For example, by entering the word 'Bean' in the author/editor field in Figure 5.2, it is possible to ensure that you retrieve books by authors with the surname 'Bean' rather than books with the word 'bean' in the title or subject fields.

Figure 5.2

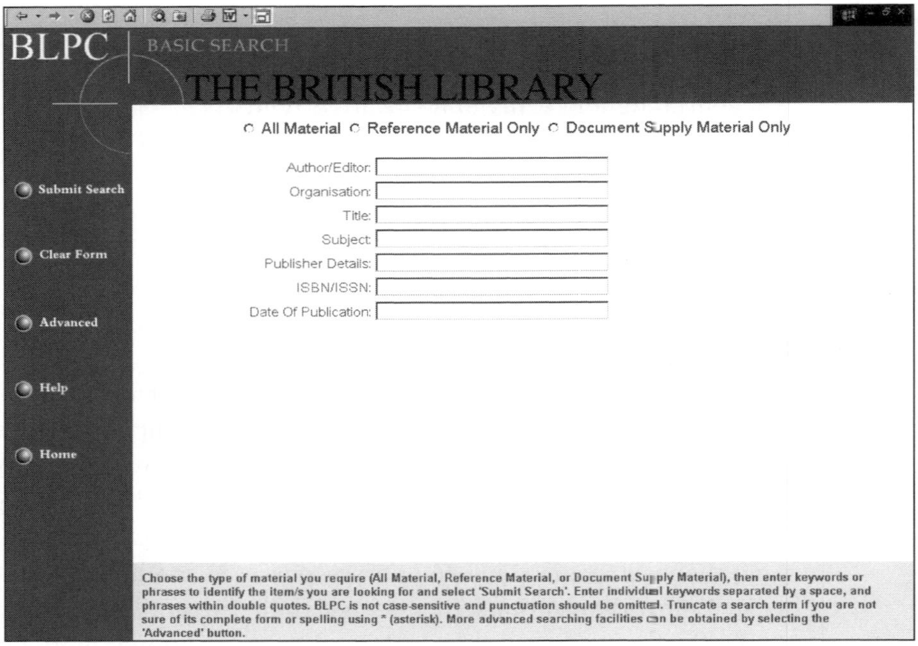

Example of a search form

The semantic web and the use of XML coding of internet resources gives users the possibility of putting their search queries into context. Many search engines allow searches to be limited to the title field of a web page, although few of the most popular internet search engines support full metadata searching. Some specialist websites such as that of the US Environmental Protection Agency do offer searches of specific metadata fields such as keywords, comments and title. Experimental work on metadata search engines developed in the late 1990s demonstrates the technical feasibility of this approach, especially when used on specific domains. The development of a general-purpose metadata search engine will depend on the uptake of metadata creation on internet pages. Current indications are that this tends to be limited to official government-sponsored websites and to educational resources provided by universities and colleges.

Collection-level retrieval

The following definition of 'collection' is a useful starting point for discussion of collection-level retrieval (CLR):

The term 'collection' can be applied to any aggregation of physical or digital items. It is typically used to refer to collections of physical items, collections of digital surrogates of physical items, collections of 'born-digital' items and catalogues of such collections. Collections are exemplified in the following, non-exhaustive, list:

- library collections,
- museum collections,
- archives,
- library, museum and archival catalogues,
- digital archives,
- Internet directories and subject gateways,
- Web indexes,
- collections of text, images, sounds, datasets, software, other material or combinations of these (this includes databases, CD-ROMs and collections of Web resources),
- other collections of physical items.

(DCMI Collection Description Working Group, 2003)

A great deal of the work was initially focused around subject descriptions and led to attempts to map different subject schemes. In the UK, the National Preservation Office managed a project to map collection strengths of a core of UK research and national library collections. This was followed by a UKOLN-run project funded by the Research Support Libraries Programme to develop collection-level descriptions (CLD). Schema such as Dublin Core can be adapted to reflect different levels of granularity using the 'relation' data element. Refinements such as Relation.IsPartOf and Relation.HasPart lend themselves to consolidations of items such as collections or parts of collections. The Dublin Core Metadata Initiative is developing an application profile for collection description and is expected to complete the current programme of work on this in 2004. It draws together Dublin Core data elements and collection-level description data elements (UKOLN, 2000).

Metadata and computational models of retrieval

Human intervention is not always necessary for indexing. Many communities of interest have explored methods of automatically indexing materials. In some areas, automated systems work in conjunction with human-applied indexing held as metadata; in other areas it is seen as complementary. Some of the automated systems work with the content of the resource (different forms of textual analysis), others with associated metadata (extracting terms from description metadata elements) and others focus on analysis of the queries to build up a user profile.

Image retrieval

There is a long tradition of automated retrieval of audiovisual material. Major broadcasters such as the BBC have established archives of television broadcasts and many major newspapers use their own or buy services from commercial image collections. These collections are normally indexed manually by a variety of criteria according to the likely requirements of their principal users. The indexing may be very specific, such as 'London Bridge', or may be general – 'bridges carrying road traffic'. The images may be indexed according to the predominant colour, for example, 'red sunset', or by some generic abstract concept such as 'tranquillity'. In Chapter 3 we discussed metadata standards such as MPEG-7, which captures a variety of attributes about a multimedia object including subject. These approaches can be developed and enhanced by deploying analysis of the subject content in different ways. Hyvönen, Styrman and Saarela (2002) identify three approaches to semantic retrieval:

- keywords from controlled vocabularies such as thesauri
- classifications using a hierarchical approach – maybe in the form of a thesaurus or a formal classification system
- free-text descriptions.

They carry this process forward by developing an ontology for a particular area of interest to provide the terminology, different views of the collection and a network of relationships that allows searchers to browse across the subject.

MPEG-7 defines other attributes of images such as format of the image file, resolution of the image, the application that originated the item and the date of creation of the image, as well as the date of subsequent changes. These are all criteria that can be used to select or to narrow down the selection of images. In other contexts the same metadata elements are used to manage the resources, as can be seen in Chapter 6. The formal metadata standards will determine which information may be available. Many image-creation packages such as digital cameras attach their own metadata to the image. In the past this information has been systematically destroyed by other databases and repositories if the image is transferred and saved in another application. Recognition of this problem means that new releases of established applications that preserve metadata attached to imported images are beginning to appear. Other metadata associated with an image includes format, resolution, originating application, date of creation and subsequent changes.

Where existing metadata is used to find, retrieve and index images on the internet, consistency of indexing and compatibility of metadata schema are an issue. The ARTISTE project (Addis, Lewis and Martinez, 2002), funded by the European Commission, deals with this by translating the metadata it finds into Dublin Core. This project takes retrieval one step further by combining content-based image retrieval techniques (to analyse features of the image such as colour and texture) with textual metadata.

Content-based image retrieval (CBIR) uses a range of algorithms for analysing different characteristics (primitive features) of images such as shape, colour and texture. This can be seen as an alternative to metadata and has been the basis for predicting the demise of metadata for images (Napier, 2001) although a combined approach has also been promoted from early on (Day, 1999). Jeong et al. (2001) go further by suggesting that the processing of images gives measures which can be encoded as metadata tags for an image. This then simplifies searching because the data has been pre-processed which reduces the amount of data processing required at the point of access. It is not clear what techniques are used for some of the major, general search engines with image retrieval capabilities, or to what extent they use metadata at any stage of the process. For instance Google indicates that it analyses the text adjacent to the image, filenames and ALT tags to allow text searching, but it also analyses content-based properties such as colouration and other attributes that may be encoded in the image such as size and file type.

CBIR is one alternative to use of subject descriptions or keywords encoded as metadata for retrieval. An object may be textual or image based, and can correspond to a web page or a component within a web page. The content-based image-retrieval approach is based on algorithms for automatic processing of images to yield measures that can be compared with an example image, or specified by a human operator. Despite improvements in CBIR, concept-based retrieval is still considered the most practical option in most image-retrieval contexts.

Text analysis and AI systems

Some systems based on artificial intelligence technology analyse the text of documents (web pages or other electronic documents) and generate appropriate indexing terms. These indexing terms may be taken from a controlled vocabulary such as a thesaurus and attached as metadata to the document or as pointers in an index. An example is latent semantic indexing.

Latent semantic indexing is derived from a textual analysis of documents that are retrieved initially in response to a search query. This is normally done by text retrieval where the search query is matched against the text of the documents being searched. The system then analyses other terms associated with the retrieved documents and does another search on the terms that most commonly occur in the original retrieved set. Using our earlier search on 'BSE' as an example, the system would look for all documents with that expression in it. Many of those documents would also refer to 'bovine spongiform encephalopathy' or to 'mad cow disease'. 'BSE' might also refer to 'Breast Self Examination' – one of the measures taken to improve the chances of early discovery of breast cancer and consequently increase the chances of survival. At this stage human intervention may be needed to disambiguate the term 'BSE' and to focus the search on 'mad cow disease'. The system then does a modified search to include relevant items that do not specifically mention 'BSE' as a term and to exclude items that might be irrelevant to this particular search. In effect the system uses the intended meaning of the term to construct its search profile.

summary

Although free text searching and Boolean logic are powerful tools for retrieval, more sophisticated statistical methods are widely used for internet searching to provide a way of ranking search results. Shannon's Information Theory and Bayesian Inference have both played an important role in the development of a new generation of search engines designed for handling large data sets. The effectiveness of a retrieval set can be measured in terms of precision and recall, one of the fundamental developments in information retrieval theory.

Although metadata is not routinely used for subject searching by general search engines, because of their susceptibility to overt manipulation by web hosts, it is becoming a valuable tool for value-added services in clearly defined domains. Two examples are the subject gateways used by the academic community for resource discovery and the Community Legal Service which provides access to legal information and advice from over 300 websites that use a common taxonomy to classify their content.

There is some debate about the relative merits of human-based indexing and machine-based indexing. Issues such as consistency of terminology and use of synonyms continue to affect the quality of retrieval and approaches such as thesaurus development may go some way to addressing these issues.

Alternatives to concept-based searching include content-based information retrieval (CBIR), which is used for analysing images automatically and using the analysis to enhance the retrieval quality. In practice some text-based indexing is also required – either by analysing the text surrounding the image, or by explicitly applying indexing terms. Another approach is latent semantic indexing which is based on a statistical analysis of the co-occurrence of terms in a retrieved set of documents in order to refine the search results and to deliver a more reliable ranking of search results.

Metadata has a key role to play in high-quality information retrieval and is particularly important in clearly defined domains. It also plays a key role in providing users with options for searching on different attributes and for putting the search queries into context. Despite these sophisticated options, many users prefer to use a simple search window where a single term or expression is entered. There is a great deal of potential for high-quality retrieval on the internet, but a lot of this will depend on educating users about the possibilities.

References and further sources of information

Addis, M., Lewis, P. and Martinez, K. (2002) ARTISTE Image Retrieval System put European Galleries in the Picture, *Cultivate*, **7**, (June), www.cultivate-int.org/ [accessed 20/6/2003].

Aitchison, J., Gilchrist, A. and Bawden, D. (2000) *Thesaurus Construction and Use: a practical manual*, 4th edn, London, Aslib, and Chicago, IL, Fitzroy Dearborn.

Autonomy (n.d.) *Autonomy Technology Introduction*, www.autonomy.com/c/content/Technology/ [accessed 28/2/2004].

Day, M. (1999) Image Retrieval: combining content-based and metadata-based approaches. Report from the Second UK Conference on Image Retrieval held in Newcastle, 25–26 February 1999, *Ariadne*, **19** (April 1999), http://www.ariadne.ac.uk/issue19/metadata/ [accessed 25/5/2004].

DCMI Collection Description Working Group (2003) *Milestones/Deliverables*, Dublin, OH, Dublin Core Metadata Initiative, http://dublincore.org/groups/collections/ [accessed 6/2/2004].

Goodman, A. (2002a) *An End to Metatags: enough already, Part 1*, www.traffick.com (2 September).

Goodman, A. (2002b) *Google Used Meta Tags Sparingly, but should you?: enough already, Part 2*, www.traffick.com (16 September).

Haynes, D., Huckle, F. and Elliot, H. (2002) *HSE Thesaurus*, Bootle, Health & Safety Executive.

Hyvönen, E., Styrman, A. and Saarela, S. (2002) *Ontology-Based Image Retrieval*, HIIT Publications 2002–03, Helsinki, Helsinki Institute for Information Technology, 15–27, www.hiit.fi [accessed 4/2/2004].

ISO 2788:1986. *Documentation – Guidelines for the Establishment of and Development of Monolingual Thesauri*, Geneva, International Organization for Standardization.

Jeong, K. T., Rorvig, M., Jeon, J. and Weng, N. (2001) *Image Retrieval by Content Measure Metadata Coding*. Poster Proceedings of the Tenth International World Wide Web Conference, WWW 10, Hong Kong, May 1–5, 2001, www10.org/cdrom/posters/p1142/ [accessed 6/2/2004].

Napier, M. (2001) Multi-media and Image Handling: the future is textless. A report on the DTI sponsored meeting on multi-media and image handling held in London in November 2001, *Ariadne*, **30**, (20 December), www.ariadne.ac.uk/issue30/dti/intro.html.

Sullivan, D. (2002a) Death of a Meta Tag. The Search Engine report, *Search Engine Watch*, (1 October), searchenginewatch.com/sereport/article.php/2165061 [restricted access].

Sullivan, D. (2002b) How to Use HTML Tags, *Search Engine Watch*, (14 October), searchenginewatch.com/webmasters/article.php/2167931 [restricted access].

UKOLN (2000) RSLP *Collection Description: collection description schema*, Bath, UKOLN, www.ukoln.ac.uk/metadata/rslp/schema/ [accessed 6/7/2003].

Chapter 6

Purpose iii
Management of information

overview

MANAGEMENT OF INFORMATION was the third of the purposes of metadata identified in the five-point model of metadata use described in Chapter 1. This
chapter describes the information lifecycle and a simplified model of this
provides the framework for describing management activities and the role of metadata in this. Metadata is used for the management of information in a wide range
of applications and the chapter uses examples from a number of sectors including:

* records management
* content management
* preservation
* library management.

Digital data lifecycles

An understanding of digital data lifecycles helps to provide a framework
for the management of electronic resources. Although metadata does not
refer exclusively to digital information (it also refers to books and other
physical manifestations of information), the majority of examples discussed
here are concerned with electronic resources, such as those available via
the internet. The lifecycle can be expressed as a series of phases:

- *Creation or capture of information* – this involves the original creation or compilation of the information, its capture onto a system and the attachment of metadata such as index terms to that information source.
- *Use* – during this phase of the lifecycle the information is accessed and utilized by a variety of consumers or designated communities of users. These may be specialist users, in which case the management of their use may extend to issues of authentication and rights management, or they may be general users where the potential uses may be difficult to predict.
- *Review* – at some stage during the life of an information source, it may be superseded or become redundant. The review process is intended to ensure that the overall information system continues to be up to date, relevant and accurate.
- *Preservation* – the integrity of the information sources needs to be maintained with proper back-up procedures and migration policies as the technology changes and develops.
- *Disposal* – following the review process the information resource may be destroyed, archived for future reference, or transferred to long-term storage, where cheap storage and maintenance is offset against lower accessibility.

There are many models of the lifecycle of digital/electronic resources, and this is a condensation of some of the key stages.

Records management

Records management plays a key role in documenting government decisions, regulating industries and providing an audit trail of transactions. Records management encompasses the management of both physical files and electronic records. Although they are on different media, many of the same processes apply to each type of record. Good records management depends on establishing the authenticity of records (among other things), which is described in Chapter 7 (pp 127–8). This section focuses on the use of metadata to manage the records lifecycle. The illustration of the lifecycle of a record seen in Figure 6.1 shows the decision points and helps to identify the actions that take place during the life of a record.

Figure 6.1

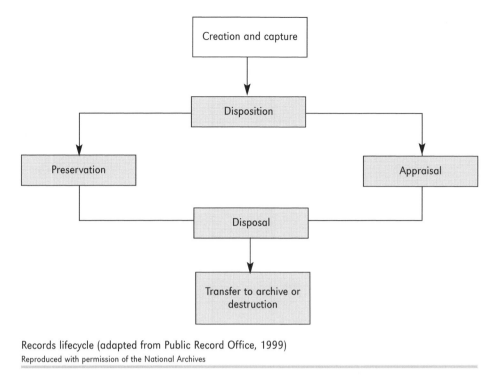

Records lifecycle (adapted from Public Record Office, 1999)
Reproduced with permission of the National Archives

A record comes into being when a document is created or received and attached to a registered file or given a file heading. During the capture process metadata is created for the record including date of creation, the owner, review date and security classification. This applies to paper filing systems and electronic records management systems and to hybrid systems incorporating paper files and electronic documents. The record may be retrieved and used but not changed. When it is due for appraisal a decision is made on whether to continue to keep it as an active record or to dispose of it either by transfer to an archive or by destroying it. The principles of good records management are embodied in ISO 15489:2001, the international standard for records management.

Some data elements specifically designed for records management have been defined in metadata application profiles based on Dublin Core. For example, the National Archives in the UK (the successor body to the Public Record Office and the Historical Manuscripts Commission) has defined a set of data elements specifically for records management in central government, but which can be incorporated into more general application profiles (Public Record Office, 2002). The 17 data elements defined by the National Archives are:

- Identifier
- Title
- Subject
- Description
- Creator
- Date
- Addressee
- Record type
- Relation
- Aggregation
- Language
- Location
- Rights
- Disposal
- Digital signature
- Preservation
- Mandate.

These data elements represent the minimum set that approved EDRM systems must be able to support – although they are not limited to these, and additional metadata elements are used for internal management of electronic and digital resources. The minimum metadata element set should be capable of being expressed in XML and a schema is being developed for this purpose.

Metadata and levels of aggregation

Manual systems for records management have always had metadata associated with them. It was usually found on the file covers, which had information on: date opened, file title, file series, owner, next review date, security classification, and in some cases a record of who had accessed the record during its life. The development of computer-based records management systems meant that increasingly this metadata was held on a database, which was used to generate review lists and disposal lists, as well as acting as a retrieval tool.

There are specific points in the life of a record that require human intervention or some kind of processing. The electronic systems can do this by means of metadata associated with the records. In the case of electronic documents some of the metadata, such as date of creation, author and version number, may be embedded in the document itself. Other metadata may be held separately in a database.

One of the fundamental principles of good records management is the idea of a record plan or file plan, a taxonomy for classifying records. This feature is supported by a growing number of records management systems and has been incorporated into functional specifications for approved systems. Many taxonomies used for categorizing records are based on functional analysis of organizational activities (and therefore of the associated documents or records). Although there are other methods of classification, such as subject classifications and organizational charts, the functional analysis has the advantage of endurance. A classification based on a functional analysis of an organization tends to endure for longer than a subject-based classification or description of records by department within an organization. The structure of organizations can rapidly become out of date following internal reorganizations. The function is usually more constant. This is particularly the case for public authorities whose role and function is often determined by legislation.

A functional analysis is based on a three-layer approach. At the top level the general functions of the organization are identified and listed. In practice this may require several rounds of consultation before they are agreed and a high-level analysis is settled on. Under each function are activities that are carried out in order to fulfil the functions. The third layer is processes, sometimes labelled as sub-activities. For example:

> Managing human resources – function
>> Recruiting staff – activity
>>> Staff interviews – process
>>> (*HSE Business Classification Scheme*, Huckle and Haynes, 2003)

Metadata can be associated with any level of the file plan and lower levels inherit the attributes of the higher level. For instance, if it is decided that all records relating to corporate policy making should be kept indefinitely, all the subsidiary records under that heading would also be kept indefinitely. This makes management of records much easier, because a decision is taken for a category of records rather than on a record-by-record basis. There is still latitude to make exceptions where necessary. For instance if it is decided that some of the records associated with the organization of corporate policy making need not be kept indefinitely (they are ephemeral), they could have a much shorter retention period than the rest of the records in that category.

The *Guidelines for Management, Appraisal and Preservation of Electronic Records* (Public Record Office, 1999) puts forward a model of an electronic record, comprising the following components:

- Document metadata – document profile
- Content – the document itself
- Record metadata – context and history.

Metadata features prominently in the functional specification produced by the National Archives in the UK – a market-creating standard for products used in the public sector. Australia, which in many ways leads practice in records management by a number of years, has also defined metadata standards as has the US Department of Defense (2002) in its records management standards, widely adopted by federal agencies and increasingly by the private sector in North America.

Content management

Boiko (2002) defines content as 'information put to use'. He goes on to explain that information includes all the common forms for recorded communication such as:

- *text* – e.g. in articles, books and news items
- *sound* – e.g. music, conversations, reading
- *images*
- *motion* – e.g. videos, films and animations
- *computer files* – e.g. spreadsheets, slideshows and graphics.

He extends the definition of content to describe it as 'information plus data'. The data referred to here is metadata (i.e. data about information), which 'makes the context and meaning of information explicit enough that a computer can handle it'.

Content management systems have three components: the collection, management and publishing of information. They are not necessarily tied to web publishing and have been successfully used for distributing information through a variety of media. However, CMS technology is mostly applied to the management of web content and it is this aspect of content management that is focused on in this book.

Website development has become more sophisticated with corporate websites often containing hundreds of thousands or even millions of web pages.

The responsibility for the content of individual areas of a website may fall to different parts of an organization. This distributed management approach requires a high level of co-ordination to avoid the following problems:

- fragmented and disjointed website, effectively made up of lots of different websites with a common domain
- broken internal links (especially following updates and restructuring of other parts of the website)
- out-of-date material caused by not being able to track individual pages for updating
- orphaned material that has been forgotten about and which has no owner
- duplication and contradictions within the overall site because of lack of co-ordination of material by the different departments and authors.

Browning and Lowdnes (2001) suggest that there are three core functions that a CMS must provide:

- Versioning – so that groups of individuals can work safely on a document and also recall older versions
- Workflow, so that content goes through an assessment, review or quality assurance process
- Integration, so that content can be stored in a manageable way, separate from web site design 'templates', and then be delivered as web pages or re-used in different web pages and different document types.

Although many of the web-authoring tools add basic metadata such as 'title', 'date created' and even the name of the web-authoring software, there may be very little information that can be used to manage the site actively.

Content management systems call on a variety of metadata elements, many of them proprietary and intended merely for internal transaction processing, some following wider standards such as Dublin Core. Web pages encoded in HTML or XML lend themselves to embedded metadata. This has the advantage of transportability and allows them to be handled by different software applications.

However, most content management systems use a database architecture with separate repositories for the metadata and the content of the resource being published. The separate metadata repositories may use proprietary standards for some of their metadata, which consequently makes it opaque to users of other applications. Figure 6.2 shows a web page with embedded metadata which may be defined by a DTD or an XML schema. There is no separate repository for metadata. Figure 6.3 illustrates a common architecture for content management systems. The metadata is held in a database which is accessible to the CMS and which points to the content. The metadata is defined by a DTD, an XML schema or by a proprietary metadata standard (an internal standard for the CMS).

Figure 6.2

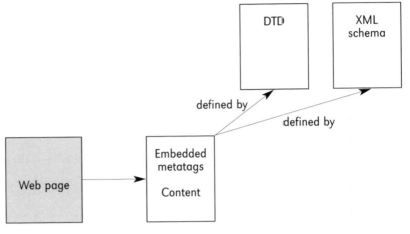

Web pages with embedded metadata

Figure 6.3

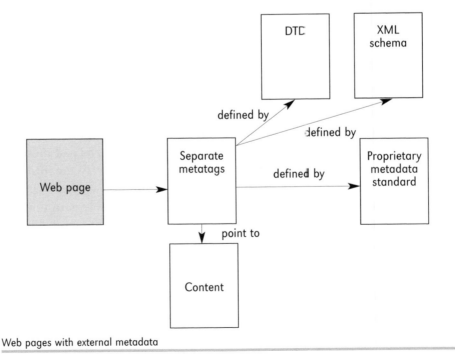

Web pages with external metadata

Metadata for Information Management and Retrieval

Metadata allows the management of content types. The workflow activities may be determined by content type and will call on associated metadata such as date of last update and access code to establish who has permission to alter the content of a particular resource. Version history of a resource may also be an important part of the process of publishing material on the web. For example version numbers below 1.0 may be the draft or pre-publication forms. A feature of many CMSs is the ability to support customizable metadata. This allows web managers to create filters for dynamic content such as 'What's new', updatable menus and topical items on the website.

Preservation

The PADI (Preserving Access to Digital Information) initiative operated by the National Library of Australia states that: 'preservation metadata is sometimes considered a subset of administrative metadata, assisting in the management of information, and technical metadata, assisting current access to the digital content' (National Library of Australia, 2003).

There are two approaches to preservation of physical materials such as paper archives and printed books: surrogacy and conservation. Surrogacy is important for physical resources such as incunabula (books from before 1500) which are fragile or which might be damaged by further handling. Digitization of the contents of a book, or archive, or the image of a museum object has been used extensively by libraries, archives, museums and galleries worldwide. Commercial picture agencies have also used this technology extensively. The focus is on images that can be viewed and retrieved but not manipulated – in the case of documents, the text is not encoded.

A digitized image or set of images will need to be managed in the same way as encoded text and issues such as durability of the medium, the readability of the file and the integrity of the image have to be managed if they are to be accessible to future audiences.

Many commentators have written about preservation management and metadata. One of the most useful reviews (Day, 2003) summarizes four different strategies available for preservation of digital resources, of which three are dependent on metadata. The strategies described are:

- *Preservation of technology* – preserving and maintaining obsolete hardware and operating systems so that the original data media can be read on them

- *Emulation* – development of programs that mimic the obsolete systems so that the experience of using the data is as close to the original experience as possible but using up-to-date technical platforms
- *Migration* – transfer of data to an up-to-date system – currently the strategy adopted by many archiving bodies
- *Encapsulation* – enclosing the original data with descriptive metadata that allows it to be deciphered and viewed.

This can be illustrated with reference to early digital projects such as the BBC Domesday Book project, which was launched in 1986 to coincide with the 900th anniversary of the production of the original Domesday Book. The BBC project used the latest technology of the day, a Phillips Laserdisc, to hold a combination of digitized images and original digital content in the form of text, sound, stills and moving images. The technology used then was specifically customized for the project and is now obsolete. The Phillips Laserdisc was an alternative to the CD technology developed by Sony which subsequently became a *de facto* standard.

One response to this challenge, as we have seen, is to preserve the technology so that the original media can be viewed in its original context. Preserving the original technology is expensive and requires operational original equipment and spare parts. It also requires the software to be maintained as closely as possible to the original state. This approach does not guarantee that the storage medium itself will maintain its integrity – so spare copies of the storage medium (in the example described this would be the laserdiscs) and the ability to write to them and read them (preservation of yet more equipment) is required. The big advantage of this 'industrial archaeology' is that future users would be able to experience the digital images in a similar way to the original audiences.

The alternative strategy is to migrate the file to currently supported media and software. In the case of the BBC Domesday project the content has been transferred to current DVD technology, making it available to a new generation of users. Metadata on the migrated medium will help to ensure that the appropriate decisions are made when it comes to the next migration. It can also be used to capture data about the original format of the material prior to migration.

Day (2003) concludes in his overview of preservation metadata that this area is relatively undeveloped compared with other areas of metadata use and that it may be some time before there is a widely accepted standard for handling this type of application. One of the benefits of metadata is its role in the management and recovery of digital materials, by providing a description of the format and technology used to create an information resource.

The CEDARS (CURL Exemplars in Digital Archives) project in the UK identified metadata as an important part of any digital preservation strategy (Day, 2002). Although metadata creation is expensive, it allows for automation of many of the processes involved in digital preservation, as well as acting as a retrieval tool and a way for creators to repurpose the data at a future date. Metadata makes it possible to preserve digital materials and is more cost-effective in the long term. If digital objects have metadata embedded in them, or are encapsulated with metadata, they can become self-documenting. It allows the re-creation and interpretation of the structure and content of digital data at a future date. The CEDARS project supports migration and emulation as preservation strategies.

CEDARS was intended to provide a framework for the development of an international standard for preservation metadata. It used the *Reference Model for an Open Archival Information System (OAIS)* (see pp 48–50) to develop the system (Consultative Committee for Space Data Systems, 2002). OAIS provides a functional model and information model for digital preservation and provides one way of handing this issue of preservation. It also provides a channel of communication between different communities that are concerned with preservation issues such as archivists, publishers and the library community.

Library management

In earlier chapters we looked at the way in which metadata is used in library management systems to aid retrieval – a way of delivering a catalogue and search facilities to users. The 'discovery' role of metadata is a crucial part of making information accessible to target groups. Library management systems also help librarians to manage items and collections and one of the keys to this is effective use of metadata. Some of the data elements associated with resource discovery will also apply to data management. For instance identifiers are necessary for searching (resource discovery) and for the management of resources during the cycle of acquisition, cataloguing, circulation, use and disposal. Most library management systems have their own internal metadata, although increasingly they are working within wider standards to allow sharing of collection responsibilities between libraries and to co-ordinate the acquisition and disposal of items. One of the keys to exchange of data is the use of common bibliographic standards such as MARC21 and adoption of XML to mark up files.

Acquisition

Co-operation between the book trade (publishers, suppliers, retailers) and the library and information community has opened up a number of possibilities. The acquisitions process can be handled electronically – ranging from the small-scale ordering of individual items via internet suppliers (e.g. amazon.com and bol.com) or direct from the publisher, through to purchase via large-scale suppliers such as Swets. Basic cataloguing data can be used to identify relevant items (e.g. author, title information). If already known, identifiers such as ISBNs can also be used for selecting titles. Publisher-supplied metadata can be made available as part of the ONIX data, or MARC records can be located from central cataloguing authorities such as OCLC, the Library of Congress or the British Library. The ONIX records allow for tracking of order information and verification of delivery and are intended to support a fully integrated e-commerce approach to acquisition. This will include the delivery and payment details as well as price and any discounts that may apply.

Cataloguing

The catalogue record used by library management systems is the basis for identifying individual items and for management. Although most library management systems can import and export data in MARC21 format, they usually have their own internal metadata standards. The internal metadata may include location information, loan records, and details about the management of binding of journals and covering of books as well as withdrawal and disposal of items.

Circulation and use

Circulation metadata is used to identify two entities: the item being lent and the borrower. The loan item metadata is normally bound up with the cataloguing information and will include data to uniquely identify individual resources. This will be more than just the title of the resource – it will relate to the specific copy of that resource, equivalent to the item level in FRBR (see Chapter 2).

There will also be a set of data about individual borrowers which will be related to the loan items. The borrower details may include data about the number of other items currently on loan, and level of access to the collection. This is particularly true of academic libraries where postgraduate research students and academic staff may have different borrowing privileges from undergraduates or visiting scholars. Some systems may keep a record of the loan history of patrons, although this is controversial in light of anti-terrorism legislation such as the Patriot Act 2001 in the USA which allows the authorities to scrutinize loan details of suspected terrorists. Data protection legislation (UK Government, 1998) in the UK means that libraries are not permitted to keep operational and transactional information relating to an individual any longer than is required for its original purpose (i.e. to manage the loan and return of items). Records are used to keep track of outstanding loans and may then be consolidated to provide management statistics. The source of the metadata about the borrower usually needs to be verified, often by providing some kind of identification and independent confirmation of address. Authentication is an important part of managing metadata and is discussed more fully in Chapter 9 (pp 164–5).

Location is a dynamic data element. For loan collections it is dependent on loan status and is normally flagged up when the system is interrogated. This type of information is increasingly being made available to library users – sometimes with an indication of the likely length of the wait for return of the item. The library staff will have access to information on the borrower, so that they can recall the item if necessary. Figure 6.4 shows an example of a public library loan record with the relevant metadata displayed, including due date, bibliographic details of the item, the identifier (in this case a barcode number) and the status/action date. The details of the borrower are displayed on a separate page.

Figure 6.4

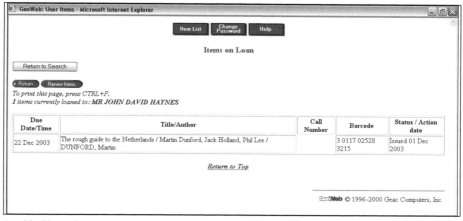

A public library loan record

Disposal

Disposal is a part of the collection management strategies developed by libraries. It is a necessary and often controversial aspect of library management. Most library collections are living collections that are managed with limited space available. One of the challenges faced by libraries is to decide how to maintain their collections in a way that reflects the current needs of the library's clientele. This means weeding material as well as acquiring new titles. Although the major national libraries are tasked with creating a repository for national (and/or language) publications, they are sometimes also faced with difficult disposal decisions. In academic and public libraries, materials become out of date, or of less interest and popularity. Books also get damaged, lost and worn out. Many reference works and texts are time limited. For instance, there is no value in keeping out-of-date telephone directories in a public library's reference section if more up-to-date versions are available.

Metadata can be used to inform the implementation of the disposal strategy. Borrowing and usage patterns captured by the library management system can reveal which items are not being used and which therefore may be considered for disposal. Metadata associated with disposal will be of two types – intention and action. Intention applies to documents that have a known life or those that have been selected for disposal. Library management systems can be configured to generate disposal lists (in much the way we have seen for records management) which can be reviewed before a final decision is made.

Managing digital resources

Libraries face the challenge of managing electronic publications as well as access to digital resources. Some of these resources are freely available over the internet; others are licensed and limit access to a defined group of users for a fixed licence period. This is a common model for electronic journals. Although there are many parallels with print publications, the licensing aspects and lack of physical access to resources and the possibilities of simultaneous and multi-site access to resources impose different requirements to those of books.

Associated with individual publications is the possibility of gathering data about users and usage patterns for digital resources. This can be viewed as metadata, or can be seen as a result of use of metadata, depending on the perspective taken.

Managing access to electronic publications is still a developing area with a number of national and international initiatives currently in place to try to find a common framework for different vendors and institutions to operate within. The main focus has been on academic libraries, where there is a large, well developed market for electronic journals. The Open Archives Initiative developed a protocol for metadata harvesting (OAI-PMH) that provides a model for data providers to expose metadata, and for service providers to harvest it (Lagoze and Van de Sompel, 2002). It is most often used to expose (and harvest) metadata about e-print collections in, for example, institutional repositories. A new range of products is emerging which covers a range of functions including licensing, password administration, payments and permissioning (for copying and printing for instance). Ebsco and J-STOR are examples of suppliers in this area as well as individual universities and consortia of higher education institutions.

Recognition of the need to develop standards, or at least a common framework to cover the administration of electronic journal access, has led groups such as the Digital Library Federation to develop initiatives to bring together the interests of different groups, such as libraries, publishers and the scholarly community. The DLF's Electronic Resource Management Initiative (Digital Library Federation, 2003) is trying to address the issue of licence tracking and access administration. Another international initiative, COUNTER (Counting Online Usage of NeTworked Electronic Resources) is looking at a range of issues concerned with monitoring levels of usage of electronic publications via different channels, by aggregator, and by user community (COUNTER Project, 2003). A code of practice focusing on electronic journals and databases will provide a basis for measuring usage levels and patterns. This will be extended to include e-books and other content types in due course.

summary

Metadata is a tool for management of information resources, whether they are electronic and available on the internet or physical and accessible via a library catalogue. Metadata enables management of the lifecycle where resources are created, modified, used and disposed of. The effectiveness of metadata is being recognized in the new generation of software applications, which utilize metadata to handle transactions. They also document processes that have taken place during the lifecycle of an information resource. This can be seen in application areas such as records management, content management, preservation management and library management systems.

For example, records management systems depend on metadata to trigger events in the lifecycle of a record. The metadata can also be used to anticipate the fate of an individual record as soon as it is created, rather than after many years when it is due for review and when the originators may have moved on or retired.

Content is 'information put to use' (Boiko, 2002) and requires metadata to establish its context so that it can be manipulated by computers. Although used more widely, content management is most commonly applied to the management of web and intranet content. The core functions of content management systems (CMSs) are to provide version control, workflow and integration of content with display templates.

Preservation is a complex area with a range of issues to be addressed including digital degradation and technology obsolescence. The use of metadata becomes particularly important for digital materials because it provides an avenue for describing the format and technology of a resource, aiding its management and recovery. The Open Archival Information System (OAIS) is a widely used framework for describing digital information resources.

The final example comes from library management systems, which use acquisition data to manage the workflow from ordering and payment for a publication through to cataloguing and making it available to users. Metadata associated with loans keeps track of individual items and assists with stock-taking exercises.

These examples demonstrate that metadata is widely used for managing information resources and that this is often based on the management of a resource's lifecycle.

References and further sources of information

Boiko, B. (2002) *Content Management Bible*, New York, NY, Wiley Publishing Inc.

Browning, P. and Lowndes, M. (2001) *JISC TechWatch Report: content management systems*, TSW 01-02, Bristol, JISC Executive, www.jisc.ac.uk/uploaded_documents/tsw_01-02.pdf [accessed 6/2/2004].

Consultative Committee for Space Data Systems (2002) *Reference Model for an Open Archival Information System (OAIS)*, CCSDS 650.0-B-1, Blue Book, Issue 1, Washington DC, NASA.

COUNTER Project (2003) *Counting Online Usage of NeTworked Electronic Resources*, Edinburgh, COUNTER, www.projectcounter.org/index.html [accessed 6/2/2004].

Day, M. (2002) *CEDARS Guide to Preservation Metadata*, Leeds, CEDARS project, www.leeds.ac.uk/cedars/guideto/metadata.

Day, M. (2003) Preservation metadata. In Gorman, G E. (ed.), *International Yearbook of Library and Information Management 2003–2004: metadata applications and management*, London, Facet Publishing, 253–73.

DCMI Collection Description Working Group (2003) *Milestones/Deliverables*, Dublin Core Metadata Initiative, Dublin, OH, http://dublincore.org/groups/collections/ [accessed 10/12/2003].

Digital Library Federation (2003) *Electronic Resource Management Initiative Deliverables*, Ithaca, NY, Cornell University, www.library.cornell.edu/cts/elicensestudy/dlfdeliverables/home.htm [accessed 6/2/2004).

Gilliland-Swetland, A. (1998) Defining Metadata. In Baca, M. (ed.) *Introduction to Metadata: pathways to digital information*, Getty Information Institute.

Huckle, F. and Haynes, D. (2003) *HSE Business Classification Scheme*, Bootle, Health and Safety Executive.

ISO 15489-1:2001. *Information and Documentation – Records Management. Part 1: General*, Geneva, International Organization for Standardization.

Lagoze, C. and Van de Sompel, H. (eds) (2003) *Open Archives Initiative Protocol for Metadata Harvesting*, Ver. 2.0 of 14 June 2002, Open Archives Initiative, 2003, www.openarchives.org/OAI/2.0/openarchivesprotocol. htm [accessed 12/4/2004].

National Library of Australia (2003) *Preserving Access to Digital Information (PADI)*, National Library of Australia, www.nla.gov.au/padi/topics/32.html [accessed 20/7/2003].

Public Record Office (1999) *Guidelines for Management, Appraisal and Preservation of Electronic Records, Vol. 1, Principles*, 2nd edn, Kew, Public Record Office, http://www.pro.gov.uk/recordsmanagement/ erecords/guidelines/default.htm [accessed 25/5/2004].

Public Record Office (2002) *Requirements for Electronic Records Management Systems, Part 2: Metadata Standard*, 2002 revision, final version, Kew, Public Record Office, www.pro.gov.uk/recordsmanagement/ erecords/2002reqs/2002metadatafinal.pdf [accessed 27/2/2004].

Stockting, B. and Craven, L. (2003) Metadata and the UK Archives Network. In Gorman, G. E. (ed.), *International Yearbook of Library and Information Management 2003–2004: metadata applications and management*, London, Facet Publishing, 109–38.

UK Government (1998) *Data Protection Act 1998*, (c 29), London, HMSO, www.hmso.gov.uk/acts/acts1998/19980029.htm [accessed 6/2/2004].

US Department of Defense (2002) *Design Criteria Standard for Electronic Records Management Software Applications*, DoD 5015.2-STD, Washington DC, US Department of Defense.

Chapter 7

Purpose iv
Rights management, ownership and authenticity

overview

THIS CHAPTER DESCRIBES the issues arising from ownership, rights management and authenticity. It starts with a discussion of why these issues are important, before going on to describe rights management in detail. The Open Digital Rights Language is introduced as an information-modelling language that describes rights issues. The Indecs system and ONIX applications are discussed as examples of rights management in the book trade. There is also a brief discussion of the way in which rights are handled by Dublin Core, Project RoMEO, the Open Archives Initiatives, MPEG-21 and GRid.

The chapter then goes on to consider provenance, starting with a general definition and then discussing provenance in the context of records and archives management. It also looks at digital images (JIDI metadata and the FILTER project), electronic documents and printed material.

The chapter concludes with a discussion of the different models of intellectual property rights.

Intellectual property rights

The protection of intellectual property rights has a major economic impact on many industries. One of the drivers for the development of metadata standards in the publishing and book industry has been the need to manage intellectual property rights effectively. They form a key part of the framework for publishing while protecting the rights of those involved in creating, performing or distributing a creative work. In most countries the author or creator of a work has the right to be identified as its owner and to enjoy the benefits of ownership. The World Intellectual Property Organization in Geneva regulates international treaties to help facilitate international exchange and trade in intellectual property.

The interests of different parties involved in intellectual property protection are sometimes in conflict and use of the appropriate metadata helps to balance these interests. Metadata provides a way of identifying the interactions between the stakeholders and can provide a mechanism for ensuring that the rights and ownership issues are properly addressed.

The ease of copying and faithfulness of reproduction of digital resources pose an enormous challenge to publishers and record producers. Every day there is news about the financial problems faced by the recording industry. Widespread illegal copying affects sales. The International Federation of the Phonographic Industry estimates that in 2002 40% of all cassettes and discs sold globally were pirate (i.e. illegal) copies worth about 4.6 billion US dollars (International Federation of the Phonographic Industry, 2003). Wholesale breaches of copyright also take place with electronic publications, software and other digital resources. The challenges are twofold. The first is establishing ownership of the rights, be they publishing rights, recognition of authorship or rights for exploitation of the resource in new ways. The second is ensuring that those rights are applied and that conditions of use are not breached – or that if they are, the breaches can be detected.

When it comes to establishing the authenticity of an item, its history becomes important – its provenance, the circumstances of its creation, who owned it, and the conditions under which its ownership was transferred. The value of an item may depend on being able to demonstrate its authenticity.

Records management and good governance depends on being able to demonstrate the authenticity of a record and to provide documentation about its history and the way it has been managed. This may include details of transactions that have taken place – who viewed a particular document and when, what changes were made to the document during its history and the measures adopted to ensure that unauthorized changes have not taken place. This provides the basis for legislation on the legal admissibility of electronic documents and whether they can be used as evidence in legal proceedings.

Rights management

Work in the late 1990s (Morris, 1999) established that there were distinct requirements for rights related to physical objects such as books and those related to digital resources. In most countries there is a well established legislative framework to deal with copyright for print publications and physical recording media. For example copyright legislation in many jurisdictions makes provisions for 'fair use' and 'fair trading' and establishes a framework for payment of royalties for copyright-cleared multiple copies.

Rights management and the relationships between rights owners and users and the intermediaries were not so clear cut for electronic publications. Rights govern activities such as viewing and printing documents as well as distribution over networks and multiple accesses. Because the legislative framework for these types of transactions is often not so well defined, publishers have had to rely on licensing agreements with their customers which are covered by contract law rather than copyright law.

The drivers for rights management include the need to:

- address the differing requirements for physical objects and digital materials
- automate rights transactions for flexibility and cost-effectiveness
- work interoperably, so that data about a publication can be exchanged between publishers
- deal with different types of materials and apply to different types of user.

Several models have been developed to help conceptualize intellectual property rights and to provide a basis for the development of metadata standards. These include Indecs and the Open Digital Rights Language (ODRL), and have led to the development of industry-specific metadata standards such as ONIX (publishing industry), OAI-rights activity (government, museums and libraries) and MPEG-21 (audiovisual materials). More general schemas such as Dublin Core also acknowledge copyright and other rights in the 'DC.rights' data element. Modelling systems and languages such as ODRL can be used to mark up or express OAI and other specialist metadata.

Open Digital Rights Language

The Open Digital Rights Language (ODRL) is described as 'a standard language and vocabulary for the expression of terms and conditions over assets' (Iannella, 2002). Terms and conditions include permission, constraints, requirements, conditions, offers and agreement with rights holders. ODRL covers both physical manifestations and digital materials. It is an international initiative to develop an open standard for digital rights management providing cross-sectoral interoperability, and is extensible. It is designed to be compatible with a number of other models and standards for rights management metadata including Indecs, EBX, DOI, ONIX, MPEG, PRISM and Dublin Core. In the ODRL there are three core entities:

- *Assets* are equivalent to resources, objects or intellectual property and cover physical objects as well as digital content.
- *Rights* cover the terms and conditions for use of the assets and will include permissions, constraints, requirements for use and conditions.
- *Parties* are equivalent to users or people and cover all types of roles from end-users to rights holders and creators. The term applies to organizations as well as individuals.

ODRL is a model that describes agreements between parties for rights over assets and their use. The language can be used to model different types of relationship and to allow for a range of interactions. For example the Permission Model from the ODRL specification (Ianella, 2002) is illustrated in Figure 7.1.

The permissions cover four areas of activity: usage, reuse, transfer and asset management. Within each area there are a number of specific activities described:

- *Usage* includes permission to display or print a resource (such as text), play a video or music or to execute a program.
- *Reuse* covers permission to modify content, excerpt material, annotate items and aggregate the resource with other resources.
- *Transfer* covers permissions to sell, lend, give or lease items. These permissions are commercial in focus and would cover the permission of libraries to lend books, for instance.
- *Asset management* covers in-house management of the resource so that it can be installed, backed up, moved, deleted and restored. These are non-trading activities, but are necessary for effective maintenance of the resource within a client organization.

Figure 7.1

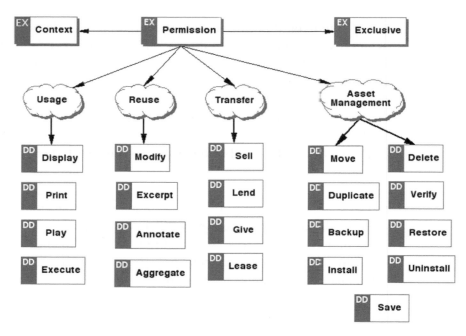

ODRL Permission model (from ODRL specification, Ianella, 2002)
Copyright © 2002 World Wide Web Consortium, (Massachusetts Institute of Technology, European Research Consortium for Informatics and Mathematics, Keio University). All Rights Reserved.
www.w3.org/Consortium/Legal/2002/copyright-documents-20021231.

Indecs and ONIX

The book trade provides a good example of the complexities that arise when it comes to managing intellectual property rights. The ONIX metadata framework was developed with this partly in mind. One of its key objectives is: 'To provide structure which can reflect the realities of national and international rights, distribution, pricing and availability' (EDItEUR, 2001). Rights-related metadata includes information on authorship, publishers and territorial rights.

In order to develop ONIX a framework was needed to analyse the different types of relationship that occur and that are necessary for commercial transactions to take place. The Indecs model is just such a framework developed with support from the European Commission with a focus specifically on rights management. It is based on the premise that: 'Trade involves rights transactions' and that 'Metadata is the lifeblood of e-commerce', thus providing a way of handling rights transactions (Erickson, 1999).

By establishing rights ONIX allows for automated rights management and for the use of rights, while protecting rights owners and allowing freedom

Metadata for Information Management and Retrieval

of legitimate, fair use. There are a number of different views of metadata, including the intellectual property view:

- Persons make intellectual property.
- Intellectual property is used by persons.
- Persons own rights in intellectual property.

These relationships can be represented by Figure 7.2.

Figure 7.2

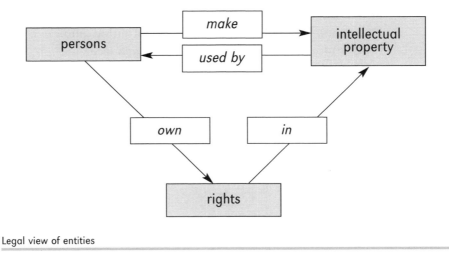

Legal view of entities

An entity such as a person may have different attributes depending on the view used. In this chapter we have looked at only one view of the relationship between persons, intellectual property and rights. Each of these entities has an identity and a function.

In the Indecs model, intellectual property is recognized as a legal concept defined by national legislation and international agreements and treaties. Indeed different types of intellectual property are defined by treaties such as the *WIPO Copyright Treaty* (World Intellectual Property Organization, 1996a) and the *WIPO Performances and Phonograms Treaty* (World Intellectual Property Organization, 1996b). Indecs actually uses metadata to describe ownership of rights, and so on, and it provides a data-modelling language from which application profiles such as ONIX can be developed. A more detailed description of Indecs can be found in Chapter 3 (pp 46–8).

Dublin Core

Dublin Core has a data element for Rights which is used to name the rights owner. Being a non-prescriptive standard DC does not specify how this data element should be encoded. Commonly the data element is used to include a copyright statement to indicate ownership of rights.

Although the rights data element does not have any formal refinements, individual authorities and organizations using Dublin Core have introduced their own refinements – such as Copyright, which would be expressed as: DC.rights.Copyright. This can be useful if there is a need to distinguish between different types of right. Another refinement is DC.rights.AccessRights to indicate intended audience and the conditions under which they may access a resource.

The scope of the rights data element is defined as follows:

Typically, a Rights element will contain a rights management statement for the resource, or reference a service providing such information. Rights information often encompasses Intellectual Property Rights (IPR), Copyright, and various Property Rights. If the Rights element is absent, no assumptions may be made about the status of these rights with respect to the resource.

(DCMI Usage Board, 2003)

Rights for research papers – project RoMEO

There is ongoing work to develop systems for dealing with rights information in different contexts. For example project RoMEO (Oppenheim and Gadd, 2003) looks specifically at the rights issues associated with the process of academic self-archiving of research papers. It recognizes the roles of author, data provider and service provider that are part of the OAI protocol. The author is the person writing the paper – often an academic. The data provider is the repository for the data and the service provider harvests the metadata in order to provide access to data in the repository. The RoMEO project refers to a number of standards including the Open Archives Initiative (see below).

Open Archives Initiative

The Open Archives Initiative (OAI) has established a protocol for metadata harvesting (Lagoze and Van de Sompel, 2003), and provides an interoperability framework which is application independent. It is based on interactions among data providers (who administer metadata) and service providers (who provide value-added services based on harvested metadata). The protocol recognizes three types of entity:

- *Resource* – the object that is described by the metadata: this may be physical or electronic
- *Item* – the constituent of a repository from which metadata can be disseminated
- *Record* – metadata in a specific metadata format.

At the time of writing (2004) there was ongoing work on the development of guidelines of OAI-PMH to incorporate structured rights information into the protocol, OAI-rights. This will work with existing rights expression languages such as eXtensible rights Mark-up Language (XrML) or Open Digital Rights Management. The main purpose of OAI-PMH is resource discovery. However, once the resource has been identified and located, access rights need to be established to allow use. The OAI-rights initiative is seen as the next logical step in this process (Lagoze et al., 2003).

MPEG-21

Looking at another type of data resource, digital images, the Moving Picture Expert Group (MPEG) has developed the MPEG-21 (ISO/IEC TR 21000-1:2001) interoperable framework for multimedia. The aim is to work across a range of communities and to facilitate integration of different models. MPEG-21 encompasses content creation, production, delivery and consumption. In order to do this 'content has to be identified, described, managed and protected' (Moving Picture Experts Group, 2001). It will be compatible with MPEG-7 which provides a framework for content description. MPEG-21 defines a framework for intellectual property management and protection (IPMP). The purpose is to enable legitimate users to identify and interpret intellectual property rights, while enabling rights holders to protect their rights. The Digital Items Declaration Language (MPEG-21 DIDL) is an interoperable schema for declaring digital items. The language can be used to represent the Digital Item Declaration model and is one element of MPEG-21 (Moving Picture Experts Group, 2001).

GRid, an example from the recording industry

Although this book is not specifically about metadata for musical recording, it is instructive to see some of the measures undertaken by the global recording industry to protect its rights. The recording industry has developed an identification system called GRid, the Global Release Identifier. It was developed for 'secure delivery of audio content to legitimate trading partners and consumers' (International Federation of the Phonographic Industry, n.d.). Metadata is an integral part of this system, and encoding is according to a published data dictionary. As well as protecting rights and allowing for trade the system also provides a mechanism for resource discovery. It sits alongside other identification systems such as ISRC, or International Standard Recording Code (ISO 3901:2001) and provides a unique identity for each release, regardless of the medium or format. Associated with each release is a set of metadata.

Rights management as an enabler

Although there are systems focused on rights management itself, it is mostly seen as an enabler that allows trade to take place. By establishing the ownership rights for intellectual property, and in particular digital objects, the rights of creators and producers can be protected and this gives them an incentive to produce and release new products onto the market. The Creative Commons (http://creativecommons.org/technology/metadata/) makes use of embedded metadata to facilitate the use of copyright material without the intervention of intermediaries. This means that an author or creator of material can make it available on the internet with standard licensing conditions. This is very useful for non-commercial material where the owner wishes to retain some rights (such as an acknowledgement of ownership) but does not require payment for use. The licence is embedded as metadata on the website or resource encoded using RDF. The metadata is in two parts: description of the work (using Dublin Core data elements) and description of the rights – such as the type of licence and the conditions of use.

Provenance

Provenance – the fact of coming from a particular source or quarter; derivation.   (*The Shorter Oxford English Dictionary*, 1986)

Metadata can provide a record of the provenance of a document and evidence that it has been kept to set standards and following defined procedures. This is vital for documents that have been scanned and digitized and where the original has been destroyed. Many banks and building societies routinely scan and digitize financial documents. The metadata associated with the digitized image helps to ensure that the resulting image is legally admissible in court. Traditionally, the authenticity of documents with legal weight such as contracts and wills was established by the signature and an identifying mark such as a seal or watermark. They also had metadata associated with them, such as details of how the document had been kept and information about the procedures in place to prevent tampering or indeed changes of any kind to the original. This principle applies to electronic documents as much as it does to paper documents.

In a Word document, for instance, the system updates details of the editing process and can keep track of version numbers, providing an audit trail. Identity numbers associated with electronic documents, digital images and other electronic resources such as DOIs (Digital Object Identifiers) are an essential part of any system that purports to preserve authenticity.

The provenance of an item of information will affect questions of authenticity and control. The value of items may be affected by their provenance. Being able to account for the entire history of a resource helps to establish that the item is authentic and not a copy or fake. This is regularly seen in the art world where a painting without the appropriate accompanying documentation is often valued at a fraction of the level of an original painting with the appropriate documentation. Although value is not necessarily the focus for digital items, their provenance or history is nevertheless an important part of establishing their authenticity.

There are different approaches to recording the provenance of an item, depending on the type of item being described:

- records and archives
- digital images
- electronic documents
- books and printed material.

These examples of provenance are described below.

Records and archives

In records management, knowing who has had responsibility for a document (especially an electronic document) is a part of the control of its integrity. Being able to develop an audit trail is a part of good governance.

This is particularly important in court cases where the documentary evidence must be authentic. The concept of 'respect des fonds' is a part of archival theory which can be used to explore the issue of provenance. Being able to trace records or scientific data (from a data archive) back to their original source is facilitated by metadata.

The UK National Archives' metadata standard for electronic records (Public Record Office, 2002), which is based on Dublin Core, has a rights data element which is primarily concerned with access rights and protective markings for public records. This may cover security levels, accessibility requirements under the UK's Freedom of Information Act (UK Government, 2000) and the Data Protection Act (UK Government, 1998), or it may determine who has access to a particular document. The standard includes sub-elements that cover different uses of the rights data element, including the following:

- Protective marking
- Description
- Protective marking expiry date
- Custodian
- Individual user access list
- Group access list
- Previous protective marking
- Protective marking change date
- Disclosability to DPA data subject
- DPA data subject access exemption
- EIR disclosability indicator
- EIR exemption
- FOI disclosability indicator
- FOI exemption
- Date of last FOI disclosability review
- FOI release details
- FOI release date.

These sub-elements are about access to a resource rather than ownership or rights management. In a commercial environment, who has access to a resource under what conditions is an integral part of rights management. The scope note for this data element specifically excludes intellectual property rights.

JIDI metadata

JIDI, the JISC Image Digitization Initiative (Technical Advisory Service for Images, 2000), has produced a metadata data structure that deals with both rights and provenance. It is specifically designed to describe a variety of visual resources and digitized images and is intended for use by the academic community. It recognizes three main entities: collections, works and visual documents. These can be related in various ways to two further entities: peoples and organizations.

- A *collection* is an aggregate of works of visual documents which have a common property. A collection may itself be made up of collections.
- A *work* is an object, such as a sculpture, a work of art or cultural artefact or an event such as a performance.
- A *visual document* is an image that depicts a work and may include a photograph of an object or a digital image.

Rights and provenance data is held in metadata elements associated with each entity. So for instance there are the following metadata elements associated with Collection:

- *Collection owner* – person or organization that owns the collection
- *Collection copyright owner* – person or organization that owns the copyright
- *Collection copyright statement* – copyright statement that appears whenever the collection is displayed
- *Collection copyright status* – the different licences for disseminating resources.

Digital images – the FILTER project

The FILTER project in the UK is designed to record information about the history of an image and its provenance. The key requirement is to record how an image is made and any changes or modifications made to the image. This is intended to help the user assess the suitability of the image for its intended use. In some situations knowledge of changes may be critical. For example, a medical image may have been manipulated to accentuate particular features and this could affect the diagnosis. Knowing what has happened to an image since it was created allows a user to evaluate its quality and significance and if necessary to recover the original image (Technical Advisory Service for Images, 2002).

Electronic documents

Legal admissibility of electronic documents and digitized images depends on the accompanying documentation and certification attesting to their authenticity. Metadata provides a way of recording details of the circumstances of creation of a document (date of creation, author, editor, etc.) and actions that have taken place since – an audit trail of who has accessed the document and any changes that have taken place, what the amendments were and who made them, when. As Chapter 2 discussed, many programs automatically attach their own metadata to electronic documents when they are created (e.g. Microsoft Word) and this can provide an audit trail for the document as it is drafted and altered.

There is no way to verify the authenticity of a document without information about its history and what has happened to it since its creation. For this, metadata is necessary. The authenticity of information can be determined by means of physical certificates to indicate that the document has been checked or that a specific procedure has been followed, or via the metadata embedded in the resource or held separately in a database.

Books and printed material

Bibliographic records can incorporate details of ownership and past history of printed documents, whether they be archives, grey literature or formally published material. Some standards allow for user-defined fields for details of ownership and circumstances of change of ownership – for example sale of an item. This type of information applies at item level (in FRBR terms) and tends to be used only for special items such as first editions of famous works, older material and items that are important because of who owned them – for instance books with dedications or inscriptions by famous people inside them. Older materials such as incunabula (pre-1500 printed materials) and illuminated manuscripts need details of their provenance to help verify their authenticity. If it is not possible to account for an item's complete history, fraud becomes a real possibility. This is an issue that museums and art galleries face with individual paintings and objects in their collections. Good metadata used in conjunction with other tools and scholarship to establish the age and origin of an item helps to build the case for its authenticity.

Comparing the models

In looking at rights management we see some similarities between different models of intellectual property rights. This is shown in Table 7.1 below, which puts forward some areas of overlap or equivalence. It quickly becomes clear that there are three main concepts that need to be represented in any model of rights management:

- *The item, content or resource* – the intellectual property.
- *The agent, party or person*, in some jargons the *user* – this entity can play a number of roles from intellectual property owner to consumer and any of the intermediaries. The agent can be an individual, a class of individual or an organization.
- *Rights* – including the terms and conditions of use as well as details of ownership and other relationships between the item and the agent.

In the Book Industry Communication paper 'Standards for Electronic Rights Trading' (Morris, 1999), the category 'User' is more specific than 'Person' or 'Party'. 'Terms and conditions' is a slightly different perspective to 'Rights'. The rights may help to determine the terms and conditions of use.

Table 7.1   Comparison of intellectual property rights models

Morris paper	Indecs	ODRL
Object	Intellectual property	Asset/resource
User	Person	Party
Terms and conditions	Rights	Right

The models are capable of a great deal of complexity as we have seen above, but the use of comparable building blocks allows for a degree of interoperability between different schemas arising from the models.

summary

Rights management metadata was developed in response to the need to protect the intellectual property rights associated with digital resources and a need to allow for the different types of transaction that take place in creating and distributing electronic resources. In order to do this, models for intellectual property rights (IPR) management were developed, notably ODRL and Indecs. The recording industry has developed its own unique identifier system, GRID, and the multimedia industry is currently developing MPEG-21 specifically focused on IPR management.

Another aspect of ownership is provenance, which can affect the acceptance of the authenticity of an item and therefore its value. It is also important in controlled environments where an audit trail of transactions may be required – particularly for official records. The FILTER project has also examined the issues arising from the provenance of digital images.

For rights management to work, the data must be exchangeable between systems – in other words, interoperable. The next chapter focuses on several aspects of interoperability including its application to e-commerce. Rights metadata is also one of the components of e-commerce systems.

References and further sources of information

DCMI Usage Board (2003) *DCMI Metadata Terms*, Dublin Core Metadata Initiative, www.dublincore.org/documents/2003/03/04/dcmi-terms/ [accessed 27/4/2003].

EDItEUR (2001) *ONIX International: overview and summary list of data elements*, London, Book Industry Communication, and New York, Book Industry Study Group Inc., www.editeur.org/onixfiles1.2.1/ONIX%20Overview%20R1.2.1.PDF [accessed 7/2/2004].

Erickson, J. S. (1999) *The Role of Metadata Supply Chains in DOI-Based, Value-Added Services*, www.icsti.org/icsti/forum/fo9904/html/#erickson [accessed 7/2/2004].

Iannella, R. (2002) *Open Digital Rights Language (ODRL)*, Ver 1.1, released 8 August 2002, Brisbane, IPR Systems Pty Ltd, http://odrl.net/1.1/ODRL-11.pdf [accessed 7/2/2004].

International Federation of the Phonographic Industry (n.d.) GRid Handbook Part 1: Guide to the Handbook, London, IFPI, http://212.134.114.163/grid/ [accessed 8/02/04].

International Federation of the Phonographic Industry (2003) *Commercial Piracy Report*, London, IFPI, www.ifpi.org/site-content/antipiracy/ piracy2003-piacy-statistics.html [accessed 7/2/2004].

ISO 3901:2001, *Information and Documentation: International Standard Recording Code (ISRC)*, Geneva, International Organization for Standardization.

ISO/IEC TR 21000-1:2001. *Information Technology – Multimedia Framework (MPEG-21) – Part 1: Vision, Technologies and Strategy*, Geneva, International Organization for Standardization.

Lagoze, C. and Van de Sompel, H. (eds) (2003) *Open Archives Initiative. Protocol for Metadata Harvesting*, Ver. 2.0, Open Archives Initiative of 14 June 2002, www.openarchives.org/OAI/2.0/openarchivesprotocol.htm [accessed 12/4/2004].

Lagoze, C., Van de Sompel, H., Nelson, M. and Warner, S. (2003) *OAI-Rights White Paper*, www.openarchives.org/documents/OAIRightsWhitePaper. html [accessed 16/12/2003].

Morris, S. (1999) *Standards for Electronic Rights Trading*, London, Book

Industry Communication, www.bic.org.uk/rightstan.rtf [accessed 7/2/2004].

Moving Picture Experts Group (2001) *MPEG-21 Part 2: Digital Item Declaration Language (DIDL)*, http://xml.coverpages.org/mpeg-21-didl.html [accessed 17/12/2003].

Oppenheim, C. and Gadd, E. (2003) *RoMEO Rights Metadata for Open Archiving Project*, Loughborough: Loughborough University, http://lboro.ac.uk/departments/ls/disresearch/romeo.html [accessed 30/4/2003].

Public Record Office (2002) *Requirements for Electronic Records Management Systems, Part 2: Metadata Standard*, 2002 revision, final version, Kew: Public Record Office, www.pro.gov.uk/recordsmanagement/erecords/2002reqs/2002metadatafinal.pdf [accessed 27/2/2004].

The Shorter Oxford English Dictionary (1986) 3rd edn, 2 vols, Oxford, Clarendon Press.

Technical Advisory Service for Images (2000) *JIDI Metadata: advice paper*, TASI, www.tasi.ac.uk.

Technical Advisory Service for Images (2002) *Metadata and Digital Images: advice paper*, TASI, www.tasi.ac.uk.

UK Government (1998) *Data Protection Act 1998*, (ch. 29), London, HMSO, www.hmso.gov.uk/acts/acts1998/19980029.htm [accessed 6/2/2004].

UK Government (2000) *Freedom of Information Act 2000*, (ch. 36), London, HMSO, www.hmso.gov.uk/acts/acts2000/20000036.htm#aofs [accessed 8/2/2004].

World Intellectual Property Organization (1996a) *WIPO Copyright Treaty (WCT)*, WIPO Publication Number 226, Geneva, WIPO.

World Intellectual Property Organization (1996b) *WIPO Performances and Phonograms Treaty (WPPT)*, WIPO Publication Number 227, Geneva, WIPO.

Chapter 8

Purpose v
Interoperability and
e-commerce

overview

THIS CHAPTER LOOKS at interoperability and what it means for applications such as e-commerce. It considers the role of metadata in facilitating interoperability and explores this in a number of contexts, including e-government, electronic records management, educational technology and library management systems. The chapter considers some of the management issues that arise from the use of metadata such as content standards, the interests of stakeholders and cost versus functionality. The chapter goes on to describe e-commerce and considers the Indecs model.

The importance of interoperability

Interoperable systems allow the exchange of information and sharing of resources. A good example is the internet, where a huge variety of resources can be viewed using proprietary browsers able to interpret marked-up HTML text. Metadata associated with an internet resource, such as the MIME data type, allows browsers to interpret content and to bring up the appropriate application or viewer to access that resource.

Interoperability has been enabled by metadata in many different communities of interest from records managers to the publishing and the music industries. This achievement has in part been due to the volume and growth of digital resources in these sectors which have provided a stimulus for e-commerce. To operate effectively, trading partners found they needed to exchange large volumes of data about the products and services being traded. These might be digital music tracks, published text, or media containing audiovisual material. Use of metadata allows the automated processing of the large volume of transactions that results from e-commerce. This has contributed to the development of common formats and standards for expressing data, as well as systems that translate data from one format into another.

What exactly is interoperability?

Interoperability is an important consideration for many systems and it is important to have a clear view of what is meant by it, before attempting to explain the role of metadata. Some definitions of interoperability focus on the storage of data in a standard format. A good example can be found in libraries where the MARC21 format is used to exchange bibliographic records between systems. This does not mean that the library management systems themselves have to store data internally in MARC21 format. Indeed many of these systems have additional proprietary metadata elements. The internal architecture of the library management system may make a proprietary data structure more appropriate. However the ability to generate output in a standard format and to import records in an agreed format allows the exchange of data between systems. For instance, in a relational database system a bibliographic record is created at the point of querying the system. The different fields comprising that virtual record are stored in separate tables. A bibliographic standard that is based on discrete records in a flat file structure may not be easily translated into a relational system.

A working definition of interoperability comes from the peer-to-peer architecture community, which says that:

> two systems are interoperable if a user of one system can access even some resources or functions of the other system. (Shirky, 2001)

This is a functional definition and does not establish the conditions that need to be in place for this to happen, for example a Z39.50 search protocol that is able to extract bibliographic information from several library catalogues.

The Indecs initiative defines interoperability as:

> enabling information that originates in one context to be used in another in ways that are as highly automated as possible.   (Rust and Bide, 2000)

This definition focuses on the information aspect and the requirement to use information in different contexts from its origin. It also highlights the automated nature of transactions. The IEEE definition of interoperability also focuses on information exchange and use between systems:

> the ability of two or more systems or components to exchange information and to use the information that has been exchanged.
>
> (IEEE Computer Society, 1990)

The above definitions lead to the suggestion that metadata may be used to facilitate the exchange of information between systems. However, the data must be capable of being used by other systems. The implication is that the data is used by different systems to achieve a common end (such as the successful sale of a product).

Metadata and interoperability

The role of metadata in facilitating interoperability can be seen in a number of contexts such as:

- e-government
- electronic records management
- educational technology
- library management systems.

It can also be used for e-commerce systems, which are described separately, in the second part of this chapter (pp 142–4. Although there are many other examples, these serve to illustrate the ways in which metadata is used to enable interoperability of systems.

E-government

Interoperability is a key component of the UK government's drive towards electronic service delivery and is a significant part of its e-government strategy. This strategy is intended to facilitate the seamless flow of information across government. The benefits are seen as greater efficiency and improved access to information and services by citizens. The e-Government Interoperability Framework or e-GIF (UK Office of the e-Envoy, 2003) has two compliance conditions:

The coherent exchange of information and services between systems.

To replace any component or product used within an interface with another of a similar specification while maintaining the functionality of the system.

The e-GIF requires UK government departments to use XML (eXtensible Mark-up Language) and XSL (eXtensible Stylesheet Language) in systems. The rationale is that this allows for data integration and management. E-GIF also provides the conditions for metadata to be used for content management and resource discovery. The British government's e-Government Metadata Standard, e-GMS (UK Office of the E-Envoy, 2004), based on Dublin Core, is a part of the e-Government Interoperability Framework, and provides a minimum set of data elements for use across government. This ensures that government websites are described using a common framework and allows the possibility for search engines to be configured to take advantage of these enriched descriptions. As well as specific government portals such as Directgov, the metadata allows searches on general sites to be configured to pull this type of government information. This is described in Chapter 4. The metadata embedded in government web pages also enables content management systems to manipulate web pages using standard data elements as well as their own internal metadata elements.

Electronic records management

Electronic records management shows some of the benefits of metadata in helping to define a market. In the UK, the National Archives has produced detailed functional specifications for Electronic Document and Records Management (EDRM) systems (Public Record Office, 2002). These include the definition of metadata elements that are intended to allow exchange of data between different proprietary systems. This is important, because of the changes to government departments that can occur over an extended period. Individual business units can be moved between government departments as a result of reorganization. As each department will make its own selection of system, there is a concern that they should be able to import and work with records originated on other systems used by other UK government departments. Selecting systems that adhere to a functional specification of this nature also facilitates future migration to new systems at a later date, thereby not tying a department to one particular system.

Chapter 6 described how metadata could be used for a range of management activities including location of records, contextual information about their creation and decisions on retention and disposal. Using a common framework to describe these elements allows records to be managed by different systems, or to be transferred from one system to another. This is particularly important for records that may be transferred from one agency to another or where an organization decides to upgrade or change its records management software.

Permissive metadata standards such as those based on Dublin Core provide a basic framework for interoperability by defining the data elements used to describe the information resource. However, additional specificity is required to ensure that compatible encoding systems are being used. For instance date information may be held in a number of formats. The date format needs to be explicitly stated to ensure that the data is interpreted correctly. Semantic information is particularly prone to variation and interpretation and the vocabulary used for describing the content of a resource must be standardized to ensure interoperability. It has been suggested (Whitehead, 2001) that certain data elements in the DoD 5015.2 standard *Design Criteria Standard for Electronic Records Management Software Applications* (US Department of Defense, 2002) needed a controlled vocabulary. The data elements in question were format, media and type, with a registration process for new values in each field.

Educational technology

In the learning technologies domain the CETIS (Centre for Educational Technology Interoperability Standards) initiative in the UK provides examples of the role of interoperability (CETIS, 2002). It and corresponding international efforts were prompted by the neglect of otherwise good educational resources because of lack of interoperability. The CETIS initiative includes several demonstrator projects that provide practical applications of interoperability.

During the 1980s the BBC sponsored the development of a microcomputer for use in schools, known as the BBC 'B' Micro. This predated the IBM PC and was one of the first initiatives to ensure that school-age children had access to IT and became familiar with its use. It also became a tool for delivery of learning and a lot of learning material was developed for this environment. However, the widespread adoption of the IBM PC and compatible technology (today's PCs) meant that the user base of BBC 'B's gradually declined to the point where they are now quite rare. The learning materials designed for the BBC 'B' have either been converted for PCs or are not used at all. Today the existence of IEEE Learning Object Metadata, LOM (IEEE Learning Technology Standards Committee, 2002), makes it possible to catalogue learning materials and to share this information in a networked environment. The IMS Global Learning Consortium has developed guidelines and good practice in the use of LOM (Thropp and McKell, 2001).

In the learning technology field existing metadata standards such as LOM and IMS allow transactional data to be passed from one system to another. This allows student information to be transferred between different applications within an institution (for dealing with accommodation, access to electronic resources and course registration details) and between institutions (if a student transfers courses).

Library management systems

Increasing use of MARC21 as a common format for exchange of cataloguing data has made it easier for systems to interoperate. This can be seen in the way shared cataloguing initiatives and union catalogues have changed since the introduction of MARC21. Initially libraries had to be able to produce their machine-readable catalogues in a common format for mounting on a central database in a union catalogue. Resource constraints mean that an alternative, distributed architecture has also developed where each library catalogue operates independently, but is accessed through a common interface. Although this is a cheaper option than a true union catalogue, the functionality is consequently restricted. Querying languages and systems such as the Z39.50 protocol enable users to search library catalogues that adhere to a common metadata standard. This allows compliant search engines to retrieve from several catalogues during a single user query. As one commentator has suggested:

> Where MARC formats differed, initiatives interested in sharing records had to map the particular formats they were dealing with. These mappings would typically be developed afresh for each initiative, although in the 1990s tools were developed to make this process easier (the EC funded a project called

UseMARCON). Obviously where MARC21 now exists, the process is made
even easier.   (Day, 2004)

Libraries also interact with the wider book trade. They are major pur-
chasers of published material and as such may also order and purchase
books using ONIX or other frameworks for electronic transactions. One
possible future development will be to consider interoperability between
library management systems and trading systems such as ONIX.

Management issues

The use of metadata to enable interoperability brings up a number of management issues:

* content standards
* suppliers' interests versus customers' interests
* cost versus functionality.

Content standards

In order to exchange data there has to be a commonly recognized format
for describing that data, a metadata standard. These standards cover not
only what data is expressed but also how that data is expressed. For
instance, an information resource may have a date field associated with
it. An example would be the date that a recording was made. An agreement on how date is expressed would be needed between two applications,
even if their internal date representations were different. Otherwise there
is room for confusion. For example, does 03/04/02 mean March 4 2002
(North America), or 3 April 2002 (Europe)? Frameworks such as Dublin
Core suggest encoding schemes, but they are not mandatory, and it is
important that the scheme is made explicit in the data itself. Using different date conventions is not of itself a problem, so long as the convention
is explicit and there is a way of converting from one format to another.
In a wider context content standards need to be agreed between metadata systems so that like is compared with like and so that the content
is interpreted in the appropriate way.

Suppliers' interests versus customers' interests

Some would suggest that it is in the suppliers' interests to keep their systems proprietary, so that their customers remain dependent on them.

Suppliers are also able to develop unique features and ways of handling data and transactions that set them apart from their competitors. Users on the other hand want the widest choice and interchangeability of systems. Once they have opted for a particular system, they want the reassurance of knowing that they can select another system and be able to transfer their data to it. They also want to be confident of selecting a system that allows them to continue to interact with other applications. The interests of suppliers sometimes conflict with those of their customers.

Defined metadata standards make possible for customers to exercise choice, by either providing a common language for output from the old system and for import to the new system, or by defining the data format used by both systems. The downside of premature adoption of a standard is that it effectively creates a bias towards one system and stops development in other areas. This issue has affected the way in which suppliers have responded to standards development work and has caused a rethink among groups such as IMS, which is now adopting a more modular approach to standards development. This means that the standards keep in line with the development of technology and that there is a phased approach to the introduction of metadata standards.

Cost versus functionality

In a paper on the role of standards in interoperability (Arms et al., 2002) the authors suggested that increasing the functionality of a standard increases the cost of acceptance and reduces the number of adopters. A similar relationship can be drawn between the functionality of a text mark-up system and the cost of acceptance. ASCII is seen as cheap to adopt, but with limited functionality, whereas SGML is very function-rich and expensive to adopt. So, for wide adoption, a standard should be cheap to adopt even though this will probably mean it will have limited functionality. A paper on the OAI (Fox, 2001) draws a similar relationship for interoperability, as illustrated in Figure 8.1. The HTTP standard is cheap to implement, but has limited functionality. Metadata standards such as the Dublin Core and OAI have greater functionality and are more costly to implement. Standards such as Z39.50 for querying databases have a great deal of functionality built into them and are also costly to implement.

One of the reasons for the widespread use of Dublin Core as the basis for application profiles is its simplicity and ease of comprehension. However, its permissiveness can limit the benefits of exchange of metadata and often does not deliver sufficient benefit for its use to be justified. This is

Figure 8.1

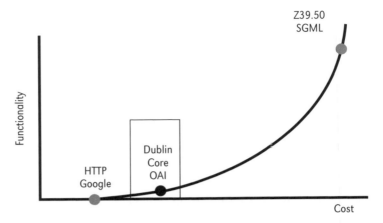

The relationship between cost and functionality
© Fox, 2001

why many internet resources are not formally metatagged. The benefit of an increased rate of transaction processing as a result of interoperable systems can be one factor that stimulates the development of highly functional metadata standards.

E-commerce

E-commerce can be defined as electronic trading and is widely used to mean online buying and selling – especially via the internet. However it is not restricted to the internet and it encompasses all kinds of commercial activity that require automated exchange of digital information in order to transact business. The focus in this book is on the supply of intellectual property products such as digital music recordings and printed books, which can be described by metadata. Metadata is used for retrieval and provides a way of enabling commercial transactions to take place. E-commerce can range from sending an e-mail message to a supplier with an order for a product or service, right through to a fully automated system that allows product selection, verification of the customer identity and secure electronic transfer of money, feeding into stock selection, dispatch systems and logistics systems for tracking an order and making sure that it reaches its destination. E-commerce systems also face the challenge of ensuring that the intellectual property holder receives royalties based on the volume of sales of their works.

E-commerce depends on exchange of data and the ability to process data received from one system and then to pass it on to another. This is essential in an environment where there are many different functions in the chain between producer and consumer and a broad range of proprietary products for each specific area of activity within the chain.

Modelling e-commerce

Interoperability can be characterized in different ways. For example, the Indecs framework (Rust and Bide, 2000) defines six types of interoperability in the context of e-commerce in intellectual property.

- *Media* – An e-commerce system has to be able to deal with intellectual property manifest in different media such as books, serials, audiovisual materials and software.
- *Function* – It should work for different functions and activities such as cataloguing, discovery, workflow, rights management, etc.
- *Levels of metadata* – It should be capable of dealing with different levels of metadata from simple to complex, depending on the requirements of the application. For instance in some contexts a book title may be sufficient to identify an item, whereas in others it may require details of the edition number and imprint and other publications details.
- *Linguistic and semantic* – Does a term used in one context apply in other contexts? For example, 'creator' may mean different things in different contexts – it could be a translator, the person with editorial responsibility, the author or illustrator of a work. The system should be capable of operating across different languages – for instance by including a language code in the data element.
- *Territorial* – It should be adaptable to different legal systems and jurisdictions, i.e. not tied to any one system.
- *Technology platforms* – It should be independent of a specific technology or proprietary system.

A good e-commerce metadata system should be able to fulfil these interoperability requirements and in doing so is said to be 'well formed'. A problem in any of these areas is in effect a trade barrier to be overcome.

The Indecs metadata framework described in Chapter 3 (pp 46–8) provides a way of modelling e-commerce transactions. The Indecs model states that 'People make stuff' and this is the starting point for rights management and e-commerce. The Indecs model also states that 'People use stuff', which means that there is a market for intellectual property including information resources. The third statement 'People do deals about stuff' is an acknowledgement that trade takes place. Although the Indecs model is intended to deal with commercial transactions, it also deals with transactions such as lending from a public library. In the Indecs model a library lends books (stuff) to library members (people) for free. Money transactions do of course occur at some stage; the library has to buy books and in some countries royalties may be payable for loans.

In order to manage the metadata associated with e-commerce transactions, the Indecs framework puts forward the following principles, which could be applied to other domains as well, and are therefore worth rehearsing here:

- *Unique identification* – 'Every entity should be uniquely identified within an identified namespace.' This ties in with Axiom 3 of the Indecs model (described in Chapter 3, p. 47), that metadata is modular and Axiom 2, that stuff is complex. Without a unique identifier for each entity it becomes difficult and expensive to administer some aspects of the e-commerce chain. The principle goes on to describe the attributes of an identifier of uniqueness, stability, security and public availability of basic descriptive metadata for the entity identified.
- *Functional granularity* – 'It should be possible to identify an entity whenever it needs to be distinguished.' This means that an item should be capable of being identified at whatever level of granularity is appropriate. For a library this may be the entire collection, or for a music recording it may be a compilation of many pieces from different artists. However, for royalty payments, it will be necessary to issue an identity to each individual work, each creator and each performer separately.
- *Designated authority* – 'The author of an item of metadata should be securely identified.' This is necessary to authenticate the metadata and to provide an audit trail.
- *Appropriate access* – 'Everyone requires access to the metadata on which they depend, and privacy and confidentiality for their own metadata from those who are not dependent on it.'

The Indecs framework forms the basis of the ONIX e-commerce metadata standard for handling works such as books, sound recordings, graphic arts and films. ONIX is described in Chapter 3 (pp 57–9).

See also Chapter 7 (pp 122–3) for a description of how Indecs could be used for modelling the relationships associated with intellectual property rights. E-commerce involving intellectual property requires effective rights management to be in place.

Interoperability allows systems to exchange information and make use of the information which has been exchanged as part of an overall transaction or process. Metadata plays an important role in enabling interoperability between systems. The role of metadata to ensure interoperability can be seen in e-government initiatives, records management, educational technology and the world of library catalogues. Indeed the e-Government Interoperability Framework (eGIF) in the UK requires adherence to a common metadata standard, e-GMS, based on Dublin Core. In electronic records management, metadata standards are used to specify systems in such as way that they can exchange data and in some cases interoperate. In the educational technology field, metadata standards such as IEEE LOM and IMS allow deployment of learning resources in different environments, as well as the transfer of student registration data between applications. The Z39.50 protocol allows interoperability between catalogues adhering to a metadata format, such as MARC21, so that users can search across several resources with a single query.

A number of issues need to be addressed when using metadata as a basis for interoperability. There has to be a common agreement about standards, not only for individual data elements, but also for encoding of data. The interests of suppliers (who tend to work with proprietary systems) and customers (who want maximum choice) need to be balanced. A balance also has to be struck between cost and functionality.

Metadata plays a key role in facilitating e-commerce, particularly in the sale of intellectual property. The Indecs framework furnishes a way of modelling e-commerce entities, transactions and relationships and forms the basis of metadata standards for e-commerce such as ONIX, widely used in the publishing industry and book trade.

The next chapter on the management of metadata considers a number of issues, including interoperability between metadata schemas.

References and further sources of information

Arms, W. Y., Hillmann, D., Lagoze, C., Krafft, D., Marisa, R., Saylor, J., Terrizzi, C. and Van de Sompel, H. (2002) A Spectrum of Interoperability: the site for science prototype for the NSDL, *D-Lib Magazine*, **8** (1), www.dlib.org/dlib/january02/arms/01arms.html [accessed on 26/8/2003].

Centre for Educational Technology Interoperability Standards (2002) *Learning Technology Standards: an overview*, CETIS, www.cetis.ac.uk/static/standards.html [accessed 25/8/2003].

Day, M. (2004) Personal communication to the author.

Fox, E. (2001) Opening Remarks and Historical Overview (ACM SIGIR 2001 workshop on Open Archives: Communities, Interoperability and Services, held on 13 September 2001 in New Orleans), http://fox.cs.vt.edu/noai/sept01/SIGIR [accessed 21/04/04].

IEEE Computer Society (1990) *IEEE Standard Computer Dictionary: a compilation of IEEE standard computer glossaries*, New York, Institute of Electrical and Electronics Engineers.

IEEE Learning Technology Standards Committee (2002) *IEEE Standard for Learning Object Metadata*, 1484.12.1-2002, New York, Institute of Electrical and Electronics Engineers.

IMS Global Learning Consortium Inc. (2001) *IMS Learning Resource Metadata Specification*, Version 1.2.1, Burlington, MA, IMS Global Learning Consortium Inc., www.imsglobal.org/metadata/index.cfm [accessed 12/4/2004].

Public Record Office (2002) *Requirements for Electronic Records Management Systems, Part 2: Metadata Standard*, 2002 revision, final version, Kew, Public Record Office, www.pro.gov.uk/recordsmanagement/erecords/2002reqs/2002metadatafinal.pdf [accessed 27/2/2004].

Rust, G. and Bide, M. (2000) *The Indecs Metadata Framework: principles, model and data dictionary*, WP1a-006-2.0, Indecs Framework Ltd, www.Indecs.org/ [accessed 5/5/2003].

Shirky, C. (2001) Interoperability, not Standards, *The O'Reilly Network* (15 March), www.openp2p.com/lpt/a/680 [accessed 25/8/2003].

Thropp, S. and McKell, M. (eds) (2001) *IMS Learning Resource Meta-Data Best Practice and Implementation Guide*, Version 1.2.1, Burlington, MA, IMS Global Learning Consortium, http://imsglobal.org/metadata/imsmdv1p2p1.html [accessed 13/2/2004].

UK Office of the e-Envoy (2003) *E-Government Interoperability Framework (e-GIF)*, Version 5.0, London, Cabinet Office, www.govtalk.gov.uk/documents/e-gif_v5_part1_2003-04-25.pdf [accessed 9/2/2004].

UK Office of the e-Envoy (2004) *E-Government Metadata Standard*, Version 3.0, London, Cabinet Office, http://purl.oclc.org/NET/e-GMS [accessed 24/5/2004]

US Department of Defense (2002) *Design Criteria Standard for Electronic Records Management Software Applications*, DoD 5015.2-STD, Washington DC, US Department of Defense.

Whitehead, J. (2001) *Notes from a Workshop on Metadata Interoperability for Electronic Records Management held on November 15th, 2001 at College Park, MD*, www.soe.ucsc.edu/~ejw/metadata/erm-workshop.txt [accessed 25/8/2003].

Chapter 9
Managing metadata

overview

MANAGING METADATA, LIKE other aspects of information management has to be appropriate to the requirements of its users and fit for purpose. If the metadata is too detailed it is costly to maintain, but if it is not detailed enough, the functionality is severely limited. Metadata must be applied in a consistent way and should be retrievable by those that need access to it. The management of metadata can be seen as a series of stages, although in most instances a user will only be concerned with one or two stages in the cycle. This chapter looks at some of the techniques used for managing metadata.

The issues surrounding the management of metadata are considered, and some of the techniques that are used for metadata management are described. The project lifecycle concept is used as the framework for discussion. The management of metadata starts with analysing metadata requirements and moves on to the development and selection of metadata schemas. There is then a discussion about encoding metadata and the use of controlled vocabulary before the chapter goes on to look at content rules. A section on interoperability of metadata schemas focuses on crosswalks and metadata registries. A quality management section then covers the use of administrative metadata and reviews issues such as security of information. The final part of the chapter looks at user education and the presentation and use of search aids to make metadata more accessible. The chapter concludes with a view on the convergence of management practice for metadata across the domains.

The project lifecycle

The management of metadata can be seen in terms of a project lifecycle with the following stages (illustrated in Figure 9.1):

- analysing metadata requirements
- selecting and developing metadata schemas
- encoding and maintaining controlled vocabularies
- content rules
- interoperability
- quality management
- search aids and user education.

Figure 9.1

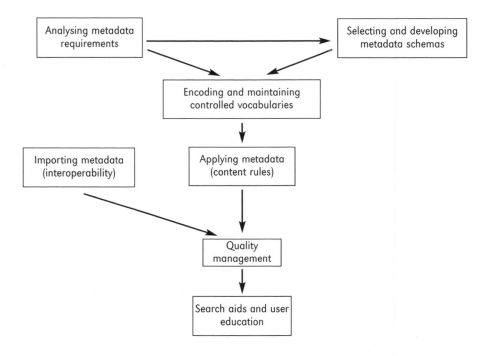

Stages in the lifecyle of a metadata project

In this model the analysis of metadata requirements sets the criteria for selecting an appropriate scheme or developing a schema or application profile. The selection may be constrained by issues such as who is using which standard, and practical issues of cost of development of a purpose-made metadata schema. The next stage is to define the vocabulary used in each of the fields (in database terms, a data dictionary). The metadata is then applied to items or it may be imported from a third party, which introduces further issues of cataloguing standards. The quality management processes help to ensure a consistently indexed resource that is suitable for searching and other user interactions. The steps are described in detail below.

Analysing metadata requirements

Although in many areas of activity there may be little or no choice of metadata schema to adopt, it is still worth establishing what the metadata requirements are. Metadata standards and practice are still evolving and new schemas and applications profiles are being developed all the time. If the choice is limited now, it may not be in the future and having a clear idea of requirements and a specification will provide a basis for review of decisions and for revisions of strategy if the opportunity should arise.

In order to manage metadata, the purpose to which it will be put should be clear. Using the five-point model put forward in Chapter 1 (pp 15–17), it is likely that one purpose will predominate, although others will play a role and need to be taken into account. For instance metadata may be used primarily for retrieval (Purpose 2), but description and identification (Purpose 1) may be other important requirements, and it may be necessary to use the metadata as a tool for managing the resource (Purpose 3).

In practice most metadata schemas have resource description as one of their purposes and they are usually utilized in a variety of ways. For instance library standards such as MARC21, while dealing with resource description (Purpose 1), are also used for information retrieval (Purpose 2) in library catalogues, and resource management (Purpose 3) in library management systems. Metadata associated with records management and preservation is an example of management of information (Purpose 3), but there is often an information retrieval aspect as well. Metadata associated with ONIX is used for both rights management (Purpose 4) and e-commerce (Purpose 5).

The analysis of requirements has to take into account what is being described, the systems it needs to interact with, the level of granularity that has to be supported, the user community, existing standards and the format of pre-existing metadata. It may also be necessary to take into account the software environment under which the metadata will operate.

Selecting and developing metadata schemas

Extensive work has been done in some domains to develop metadata schemas that are appropriate to a particular community of users. Table 9.1 summarizes some of the existing schemas that are specific to particular domains.

Table 9.1   Metadata schemas and domains

Schema and modelling languages	Domain or purpose
IEEE Learning Object Metadata	Education
Australian Government Locator Service	Government
E-Government Metadata Standard	Government
Government Information Locator Service	Government
JPEG-2000	Images
Machine-Readable Cataloguing (MARC)	Libraries
Moving Picture Expert Group MPEG-21	Multimedia
Moving Picture Expert Group MPEG-7	Multimedia
ONIX	Publishing industry
Extensible Rights Metadata Language (XrML)	Rights management
Indecs	Rights management
Open Digital Rights Language (ODRL)	Rights management
Dublin Core Metadata Element Set	Web

A listing of schemas was established by the SCHEMAS project (Dekkers et al., 2001) and can be viewed on the SCHEMAS website (www.schemas-forum.org). This has been carried forward in the CORES project.

The extent to which a schema is used and accepted by a community of interest will also affect the choice of metadata schema. If there is a *de facto* industry standard or a formal ISO standard this should be taken into account. In some instances the standard may be mandatory. For instance in the UK, Government departments and local authorities are required to use the e-GMS standard for metadata for web-based resources. However, there may be wider requirements of the application area itself or specialist requirements that a mandatory standard may not be sufficiently detailed to address, in which case the standard becomes one of a number of requirements that should be taken into account. Working with partners, for instance other members of a cataloguing union for libraries, or trading partners in the publishing industry, will focus the choice of schemas on those that are widely adopted within the industry. For the book trade this could mean the ONIX system or application profiles based on ONIX. Libraries often use MARC21 as a common format for metadata especially for exchange of data or searching across different catalogues, and the ability to handle MARC records is a feature of many library management systems. Future requirements for exchange or sharing of data with partners need to be taken into account. While one should not necessarily feel restricted to choosing the same schema as partners, the schemas need to be interoperable – as does the data itself. If there is already a large repository of metadata available that can be imported, this will also affect choice. Some formats have in effect become standards, and the ability to import the metadata could help keep down the potential costs.

There is the danger of over-specifying metadata requirements. There is a cost associated with creating each piece of metadata and the more detailed and complex that data, the more expensive the system will be to set up and to maintain. If detailed indexing or cataloguing is required, this is very expensive in terms of human time and effort. In some environments, such as e-commerce, it may be appropriate to create and maintain very detailed records, because of the benefits associated with automating numerous individual transactions. Compromises may also have to be made between the availability of pre-existing data which would be difficult or expensive to create but which may be beyond immediate requirements.

There are other considerations when selecting and developing metadata schemas:

- Whatever the primary purpose of the metadata, there will usually be a requirement to be able to identify individual elements and to retrieve items described by the metadata. Some metadata schemas are geared to support search and retrieval capabilities.
- Perhaps some data needs to be held in a secure environment, to protect personal privacy for instance, or needs to be secure against unauthorized access and interference. This is a particular issue for e-commerce systems. The security and authentication capabilities built into the schema will affect the choices available.
- Which metadata standards are stable and which rapidly evolving? In the case of those that are evolving, are they backwards compatible, so that old metadata is still valid?
- Is the schema available expressed in mark-up languages such as XML or as RDF?

Application profiles

Many metadata schemas encourage users to adopt standard metadata elements that are appropriate to their needs. However, additional data elements can be created to fulfil specific requirements of the application. It is also possible to adopt metadata elements from different schemas using a 'mix and match' approach. An example of an application profile for libraries is described in a recent article in *Catalogue & Index* (Holland, 2003).

Encoding and maintaining controlled vocabularies

One of the strengths of metadata schemas such as the Dublin Core is that they provide a means of comparing the content of data elements for different resources. Each element has a defined meaning so that there is a semantic relationship between them. This means, in the case of Dublin Core for instance, that the Creator data element will contain information about the person, group or organization responsible for creating the resource. This provides a mechanism for implementing the semantic web, where like can be compared with like. However, unless there is some agreement about how that data is expressed, the benefits are limited. This can relate to fundamental attributes of data such as what language it is expressed in. For instance the following marked-up text indicates that the content of the data element is in English:

```
<meta name="DC.Title" xml:lang="en-gb"
content="Home ownership"/>
<meta name="DC.Creator" xml:lang="en-gb"
content="Shelter, England"/>
<meta name="DC.Subject" xml:lang="en-gb"
scheme="LAMS-CCS"content="Home ownership"/>
```

In the case of subject retrieval an indexer may have to select terms from a controlled vocabulary such as a thesaurus or from classes in a classification scheme or taxonomy. This is especially important when dealing with a structured collection of material where it is necessary to reliably and consistently retrieve relevant material according to search criteria established at the point of need. Using a controlled vocabulary ensures more consistent retrieval. This limits the searcher to a preferred term choice rather than having to think of what synonyms might describe the concept being searched for. In records management systems a file plan provides a similar mechanism, allowing users to select files according to a designated category which may be subject based or alternatively based on a functional analysis. The selection of terms or categories can be presented as drop-down lists, as searchable databases or as navigable networks of terms.

Many specialist organizations have developed their own thesauri, tailored to their needs. This approach has also extended to EDRM systems where subject retrieval is a key consideration. A thesaurus allows a range of relationships between terms to be included. A full treatment of thesaurus development can be found in *Thesaurus Construction and Use* (Aitchison, Gilchrist and Bawden, 2000).

If a controlled vocabulary is necessary (sometimes a controlled vocabulary is not appropriate – for instance in titles or in a description or summary, where the author will use his or her own words and there is no control over the input) there are three options:

- *Adopt an external controlled vocabulary* – If a similar organization has developed its own thesaurus, or there is a thesaurus covering your organization's areas of activity, then this may be a cost-effective approach. It saves the effort of generating your own terminology and has the advantage of being in line with at least one other organization. The disadvantage is that you have no control over the development of the thesaurus and incorporation of new terms.
- *Select pre-existing standards* – There are standards for encoding particular types of data such as dates (ISO 8601:2000) and languages (ISO 639-1:2002). By their nature they are widely adopted, as they tend to reflect a consensus across a wide range of users. This approach tends to work for very specific and clearly delimited areas.
- *Create controlled vocabulary* – This is the most ambitious and expensive option as it requires an analysis of the subject coverage and functions of the organization, and considerable effort to compile. It has the advantage of being tailored to the needs of your organization and of being under your control – so you decide what new terms are added or which are the preferred terms. The disadvantage is the cost of development and the need to maintain the system.

There are many tools for developing and maintaining controlled vocabularies (thesauri) and taxonomies. A good starting point for identifying appropriate software is the Willpower website (www.willpowerinfo.co.uk). There is also a specialist 'taxonomy' discussion list (www.jiscmail.ac.uk/lists/TAXONOMY.html) which is a useful source of advice. Development of a specification for the appropriate tool can be helpful when gathering information from suppliers and selecting an appropriate package.

See also Chapter 5 (pp 89–91) for more about thesauri and taxonomies.

Content rules

When applying metadata, consistency is important. The metadata may be applied manually or may be partially automated (based on the recognition of synonyms in the text) and it may be embedded in the resource or kept in a separate database or repository. Not all elements can be populated from a limited, controlled list of terms. For instance personal names, company names and addresses are all variable, but still need to be quoted consistently. A set of cataloguing rules or conventions can help to ensure that a particular name appears in a consistent form and that users, provided they know the cataloguing conventions, can easily find appropriate entries. Of course libraries use authority lists for standard forms of names or construct them using cataloguing rules such as AACR2 or ISAAR(CPF).

It is easy to see the difficulties that can arise if there is no established convention for expressing names. For example J. Smith could be expressed as Dr Smith or as Smith, Jane, each of which will affect the filing order. More serious though is the difficulty of searching. A catalogue system may not recognize 'Jane Smith' if it files author names by surname. A search on 'Smith, J' would yield names around that search term. Figure 9.2 illustrates the sort of name variations that can occur in a library catalogue.

If the data is to be processed automatically, the parts of the name and the order in which they appear can be critical. For identification purposes it may be necessary to compare two records, and if they use different conventions, comparison becomes more difficult. In other applications, it may be necessary to know the title of the person (to send them a letter for instance), or the form may need to be compatible with another system – for data import and export.

Creating metadata values is a key management issue. Some systems, such as EDRM systems, depend on users creating their own metadata, combined with some automatic metadata creation. When a new electronic file or record is created, the responsible person has to select a category for that file from the file plan or classification scheme. That person will probably also create a title and may add keywords to enrich the indexing of the file so that others can find it in future. Some information, such as the date the file was opened, the name of the person opening it, and the department, will be generated automatically by the system.

Figure 9.2

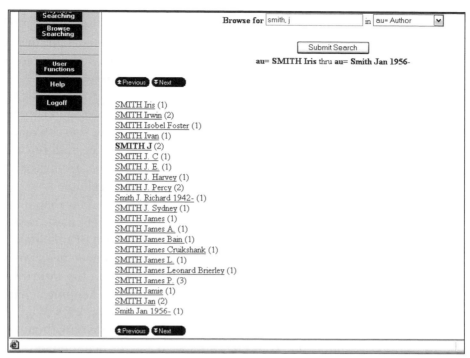

Screenshot of a library catalogue showing name variation

Some systems now incorporate features that allow for the automatic generation of metadata – so, for instance, a textual analysis will result in the creation of keywords from a controlled vocabulary, which is presented to searchers when they want to identify and retrieve a file (see Figure 9.3).

Figure 9.3

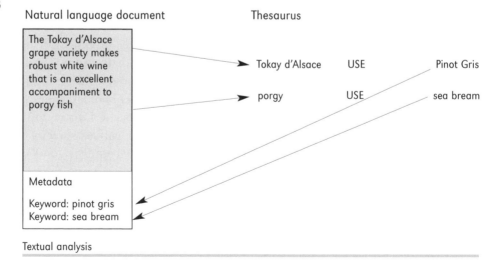

Although indexing can be done by the author of a document and index terms can also be generated automatically by some systems, for highly structured systems such as library catalogues, professional indexing can give a better-quality, more consistent result. This is expensive, because of the cost of human involvement, and it is not always possible to make this level of invest-ment. Alternatives such as latent semantic indexing and automatic analysis of text to construct indexes are offered by some search engines to bypass the need for human-intervention indexing. For certain technical informa-tion such as format data associated with images, for instance, automatic capture of embedded metadata may be more reliable.

Intelligent searching systems that 'learn' users' information requirements provide another route to accurate and comprehensive retrieval of rele-vant material. This is an alternative to the use of metadata to describe a resource and works well where individual needs are constant and the sources being searched are very diverse (as on the internet).

It is possible to manage individual items by keeping separate records on a database, and this is widely done by repositories of large collections of material. In effect the databases contain metadata about the resources in the collection. The other approach is to attach metadata to each item, so that whoever has a copy of the resource also has the metadata asso-ciated with it. This facilitates local management as well as the transfer of resources between different repositories. Networks of repositories work-ing in co-operation can develop sophisticated back-up, migration and storage strategies to ensure that secure copies of the resources are maintained while keeping storage requirements to a minimum.

Interoperability

Metadata can be imported from other sources or repositories. For exam-ple, many libraries import bibliographic records rather than cataloguing new acquisitions. This has been the basis of co-operative cataloguing activ-ities and the creation of union catalogues. This often means purchasing records from cataloguing authorities such as the Library of Congress or the British Library, or from cataloguing co-operatives such as OCLC, RLG, WLN and CURL. Importing catalogue records requires good selection pro-cedures, quality control and adherence to a common data standard.

Normalizing data

With the proliferation of resource discovery services and collections of metadata, consistency of metadata has become a major issue. One response to this is to normalize metadata from different sources. This means that it will be necessary to use the least specific data available. Although there is a loss of precision, this is compensated for by the wider range of potential sources that can be called upon.

A second approach is to require everyone to adhere to the same standard. This makes sense in communities that have very specific requirements and where there are benefits to be gained from the additional effort required. However, this approach is not appropriate for a heterogeneous community where requirements and purposes may differ quite radically.

Importing metadata from other repositories does raise a number of issues. The iLumina project (McClelland et al., 2002) identified the following issues:

- *Missing elements* – There is no control over the quality of external data and if critical data is missing from a data element, this can affect the interoperability of the resulting service.
- *Reconciling values from different vocabularies* – If two data providers use different thesauri for subject terms this will affect retrieval. Use of different encoding schemes for structured data such as dates can cause ambiguities and errors unless there is a way of declaring the encoding scheme and of translating between different schemes.
- *Lack of conventions for using or altering external metadata* – It is not always clear whether permission is given to re-use someone else's metadata.
- *Different field sizes* – If the imported data field size is larger than the maximum for the repository it is being imported to, there will be problems of data integrity and this could cause errors to be reported.
- *Inaccurate data* – This again relates to the fact that there is no control over metadata that originates externally.

Some of these issues are addressed in well developed markets for exchange of metadata and where there are widely accepted standards. For bibliographic records there is a well established market and reputable suppliers that provide good-quality data. Even so there can be variations in the level of cataloguing undertaken. In other fields it will be necessary to work with some sample data to establish the feasibility of importing it and to assess its quality and suitability before undertaking a full-scale import project.

METS and metadata interchange

The Metadata Encoding and Transmission Standard, METS (Library of Congress, 2003), is designed to facilitate the interchange of metadata on digital objects between libraries. This represents a possible way of addressing some of the issues raised by importation of metadata from external sources. A METS document consists of seven sections:

- METS header – metadata describing the METS document itself
- descriptive metadata – metadata about a resource external to the METS document (e.g. a MARC record)
- administrative metadata – information about how the files were created and stored, intellectual property rights and the provenance of files comprising the digital library object
- file section – all the files that comprise all electronic versions of the digital object
- structural map – outlines a hierarchical structure for the digital library object
- structural links – hyperlinks between nodes in the structural map
- behaviour – used to associate executable behaviours with content in the METS object.

Crosswalks

Reconciling metadata created in different environments is a major challenge and some effort has been devoted to mapping equivalent metadata elements between different metadata schemas. These mappings can be displayed as tables and are known as crosswalks. They can be used within systems to effect transformations between metadata objects. In the area of bibliographic standards, FRBR provides a model for bibliographic data that can help with the creation of crosswalks between schemes. The Library of Congress initiated some work on this to provide a mapping of MARC data elements on to the FRBR model and MARC on to AACR2.

Crosswalks have been published between Dublin Core and many other major metadata schemas such as MARC21. Table 9.2 shows an extract from a MARC to Dublin Core crosswalk.

Table 9.2   Extract from a MARC to Dublin Core crosswalk (from Network Development and MARC Standards Office, Library of Congress, 2001)

DC Element	MARC Fields	Implementation notes
Title	245	
Creator	100, 110, 111, 700, 710, 711 720	See Appendix 1 below; Contributor element not used.
Subject	600, 610, 611, 630, 650, 653	
Description	500-599, except 506, 530, 540, 546	
Contributor		See Appendix 1 below; Contributor element not used.
Publisher	260ab	
Date	260$c	
Type	Leader06, Leader07 655	See Appendix 2 for Leader-Type rules.
Format	856$q	
Identifier	856$u	
Source	786ot	
Language	008/35-37 546	
Relation	530, 760-787ot	
Coverage	651 752	
Rights	506, 540	

Crosswalks are a starting point for assessing the suitability of data sources for import. Published crosswalks provide a means of analysing the steps for data conversion that will be required. A general list of crosswalks is available at www.ukoln.ac.uk/metadata/interoperability/.

Metadata interoperability

There are two contexts for metadata and interoperability: metadata as a tool to facilitate exchange of information between interoperating systems, and interoperability of metadata schemas themselves, which can help to facilitate systems interoperability. Weibel (1998) suggests that there are three different types of interoperability: semantic, structural and syntactic. They are defined as follows:

- *Semantic interoperability* – 'achieved through agreements about content description standards'; AACR2 and Dublin Core are both examples of semantic interoperability.

- *Structural interoperability* – a data model such as RDF (resource description framework) that is used for specifying semantic schemas.
- *Syntactic interoperability* – an example is XML which provides a syntax for expressing metadata; it is about how to mark up and tag data to enable it to be exchanged and shared with other applications.

These are all necessary for two metadata systems to be interoperable.

An article in *D-Lib Magazine* (Arms et al., 2002) put forward three levels of digital library interoperability. These can be applied to other domains:

- *Federation* – where metadata from different sources conforms to a particular standard and is kept up to date. This can be expensive to implement and so tends to be used where there are significant benefits. An example of this is the interoperability of library catalogues adhering to Z39.50.
- *Harvesting* – where each participant makes metadata about its collection available in a simple exchange format. The data is harvested by service providers. This is good for heterogeneous services. An example is the OAI – this is considered less expensive for participants and is suitable for wider participation.
- *Gathering* – used for publicly available metadata, such as that gathered by search engines on the web. This is the lowest cost option for the data providers, because no additional effort is required. An example quoted is the ResearchIndex service on the internet.

The proliferation of metadata standards developed by different, and often overlapping, communities of interest means that there is a significant danger of not being able to exchange metadata. With interoperability in mind there are two sets of opposing pressures on metadata communities. The first is to simplify the standards as much as possible to ensure that the widest community can use the standard with minimum effort. This approach has been adopted by the Dublin Core Metadata Initiative. Extensions and refinements are supported by this approach, while maintaining the integrity of a core set of data elements. The second pressure is to make the metadata standard sophisticated enough to encompass the full range of data-handling requirements that are likely to be required. This is particularly applicable where the metadata is not only used for resource discovery, but also to manage the resource and to process transactions connected with the data entities being described. The

ONIX standard used in publishing and widely used for e-commerce applications and MARC21 in the library domain are good examples of this more comprehensive approach to defining metadata elements.

Metadata registries

One response to the growth in the number of metadata standards has been the development of metadata registries. The European Union and the International Federation of Library Associations and Institutions (IFLA) have developed information sources, registries and forums for exchange of information about the range of metadata standards and activities that are currently available.

One of the most important of these was the SCHEMAS project funded by the European Commission, which ran from 2000 to 2002. The SCHEMAS Metadata Watch reports (Dekkers et al., 2001) provided a quarterly review of progress with metadata initiatives worldwide. The project was intended to provide implementers of metadata with information on available schemes and standards so that they could select the most appropriate approach. It also set out to inform those involved in metadata standards activities about other initiatives in order to encourage harmonization, focusing on schemas for the following communities of interest:

- audiovisual domain
- cultural heritage domain
- educational domain
- publishing domain.

DIFFUSE was also a European Commission initiative. It provided a single point of entry to current references and guidance information on standards and specification that facilitate electronic information exchange. It supported participants in the European Commission's Information Society Technologies programme and Research Technologies Development communities.

Building on the SCHEMAS project, the European Union funded the CORES project from 2002 to 2003 'to encourage the sharing of metadata semantics'. The project established a Metadata Standards Interoperability Forum to discuss the practical considerations arising from operation across standards. It specifically supported the establishment of registries of metadata schemas to encourage sharing and re-use of existing standards. Blanchi and Petrone (2001) describe the development of a distributed interoperable metadata registry which is based on a middleware framework that tolerates heterogeneity rather than trying to normalize the metadata.

The role of interoperability

Importing metadata raises issues about the choice of schema. A number of registries and crosswalks are available which can help with the selection of appropriate schemas and therefore of potential sources of metadata.

As convergence takes place between different domains of activity – music, videos, books, digital images, electronic publications – there will be new challenges to establish interoperability between domain-specific metadata schemas and applications profiles. Hunter and Lagoze (2001) suggest that a new web metadata architecture based on the best features of RDF and XML can enhance interoperability between application profiles.

Quality management

The quality management process ensures that the metadata is consistent, accurate and complete. There are many measures of information quality that can be applied to metadata. The concept of quality can be applied to the content of metadata elements as well as to the administrative metadata. The emphasis tends to be on quality management as a process that applies throughout the lifecycle of information rather than as a check at an end point. A good outline of the history of quality management of information is given in the DESIRE project report (Hofman and Worsfold, 1998).

Quality of the metadata content

The quality of the metadata content is judged on the basis of some of the same principles as the quality of information itself. The consistency of the metadata, not only with itself but between resources, is important if retrieval is to be consistent and reliable. For instance the use of an encoding scheme will help to ensure that the contents of a particular field or data element are comparable across a resource or collection of information. Clearly an encoding scheme is in itself not sufficient to assure the quality of metadata. The skill of the human operator or indexer will also have an effect on the overall quality and therefore effectiveness of the metadata for retrieval purposes.

Administrative metadata

Administrative metadata shows when the metadata was created or updated and its origin. Its purpose is to provide a means of managing metadata (as opposed to the resources described by the metadata). The Dublin Core Metadata Initiative has defined an element set for the management of metadata known as Administrative Components. It defines the following elements (grouped by category).

Metadata for the entire record
Identifier
Scope
Comment
Metadata Location
Language
Rights Ownership
Valid Date Range
Handling specification

Metadata for update and change
Activity
Activity.Action
Activity.Name
Activity.Email Address
Activity.Contact Information
Activity.Date
Activity.Affiliation

Metadata for batch interchange of records
Database
Transmitter
Filename
Technical Format
Character Set
Bibliographic Format
Address of Result File.   (Hansen and Andresen, 2003)

A useful model of administrative metadata is the A-Core model (Iannella and Campbell, 1999) which describes the relationship between what is now known as administrative metadata and content metadata:

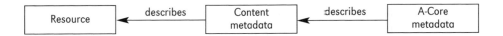

Although the original internet draft of the model has not been updated, many of the ideas in this paper have been carried forward in the Dublin Core DCMI Administrative Components, described above. The A-Core elements are divided into four components:

- Who What When
- Validity Dates
- Metadata Location
- Rights Ownership.

Security

Security is a major consideration in an interoperable environment. A useful analysis by the New Zealand government (New Zealand e-Government Unit, 2001) suggests that security is a key issue:

- to guarantee integrity of data
- to make data manageable by grouping by agency or user
- to prevent alteration of data by other agencies
- to control access to system functions.

At a basic level a security strategy for metadata will need to ensure that the metadata maintains its physical integrity, by being stored securely on a system with regular back-ups. The choice of storage medium will be subject to all the same considerations that would apply to any kind of electronic data: the robustness of the storage medium, the possibility of corruption of data by decay of the medium, storage conditions for the medium, durability of the medium, and the technology used to read the medium. A strategy for back-up and migration of the metadata will go some way towards addressing these concerns.

It will be necessary to restrict editorial access to metadata to authorized personnel. The access is usually controlled by the operating system. At a crude level it can be used to allow only certain people access to the metadata management application. Many applications that handle metadata or depend on metadata for data management have different levels of access and authorization. These typically include:

- *Read* – can view metadata and print it off – in some cases this will extend to the issue of whether or not the user even knows that the record exists.
- *Create* – can create new metadata records.
- *Edit* – can amend or edit existing records – normally the date of any changes and the name of the person making the change is recorded.
- *Delete* – can remove a record from the system – although an audit trail should indicate that this has been done.

The levels of access can be fine-tuned so that individual records or even data elements may have their own security levels. Users are then assigned a security authorization that allows them appropriate access to records or data elements.

These measures depend on the ability to identify individual users and to control their access to the system. Most commonly a user identity and password provides a basic level of security. More sophisticated systems may require some kind of physical verification such as a key. This may be an electronic key such as a swipe card, or could be based on a physical attribute of the user such as a fingerprint or iris image.

Another aspect of security is maintaining the privacy of the data. If it is being stored as a back-up on a removable medium, for instance, or being transmitted from one location to another, it may be necessary to encrypt the data. This is particularly important for data carried over the internet.

Search aids and user education

The effective presentation of metadata enhances its usability. A key aspect of presentation is the ease of navigation and searching. The navigation system and search facilities have to accommodate the needs of different kinds of users. Some people interact with systems when they create a new document and they will need to create the metadata. Other users will be primarily interested in using metadata to retrieve electronic resources, in other words they are searchers.

When entering metadata an author may need access to a controlled vocabulary, in order to select appropriate keywords. The terms can be presented in a number of ways:

- *A drop-down list* – This method is suitable for short lists of terms, or where there is a very limited number of possible options. It allows users to see immediately the full range of choices available and so helps them to select the most relevant items.

- *A navigable classification scheme* – This is more appropriate for a longer list of controlled terms, where they can be categorized according to a classification scheme. Some applications that support thesaurus relationships can display terms in a hierarchy. This allows users to navigate through the classification until they find the appropriate term(s).
- *A search* – The user enters the term into a search box and is presented with an alphabetical listing centred on the point of the search term entered. They can then browse the area and select the appropriate terms.
- *An automatic indexing system* – Some systems offer automatic indexing capabilities. In effect the system examines the resource being described and suggests appropriate indexing terms. This technique can be used for keywords or subject descriptions, where the system refers automatically to a thesaurus of controlled terms as described earlier.

General users or searchers can interact with electronic systems using the first three options to identify relevant search terms or selection criteria for the metadata, and ultimately the resource that is described by the metadata.

User education

Although there is increasing awareness of the existence of metadata, many in the user communities will not understand how metadata works. At the most basic level there will be a need to identify which metadata fields are available for searching. If the content of the fields is controlled (either by cataloguing rules or by use of controlled vocabulary), users need to know where they can browse the available keywords or terms. More sophisticated searching will require an understanding of the ways in which search queries can be combined so that, for instance, it is possible to search for the author and title of a book on Amazon, or to search for the subject category and date of creation of a web page on a government portal.

summary ▌

Metadata is an information resource and as such can be described in terms of a lifecycle with specific activities and processes at each stage:

- *Analysing metadata requirements* – this will be determined by the main purpose (or purposes) of the metadata.
- *Selecting and developing metadata schemas* – factors such as the nature of the data being described, the community using it, and pre-existing conventions and standards need to be taken into account.
- *Encoding and maintaining controlled vocabularies* – many metadata standards do not specify what encoding is used. Controlled vocabularies can be developed and maintained using thesaurus techniques.
- *Applying metadata* – cataloguing rules can be used to ensure consistency in the way in which metadata is applied.
- *Importing metadata* – the choice of source of metadata to import will depend on factors such as the quality of data available and its compatibility. Crosswalks and metadata registries provide a means of mapping between different schemas.
- *Quality control* – issues such as security are an important way of maintaining the integrity and therefore quality of data.
- *Search aids and user education* – making users aware of the options available helps them to exploit data sources more effectively.

References and further sources of information

Aitchison, J., Gilchrist, A. and Bawden, D. (2000) *Thesaurus Construction and Use: a practical manual*, 4th edn, London, Aslib, and Chicago, IL, Fitzroy Dearborn.

Arms, W. Y., Hillmann, D., Lagoze, C., Krafft, D., Marisa, R., Saylor, J., Terrizzi, C. and Van de Sompel, H. (2002) A Spectrum of Interoperability: the site for science prototype for the NSDL, *D-Lib Magazine*, **8** (1), www.dlib.org/dlib/january02/arms/01arms.html [accessed 26/8/2003].

Blanchi, C. and Petrone, J. (2001) Distributed Interoperable Metadata Registry, *D-Lib Magazine*, **7** (12), www.dlib.org/dlib/december01/blanchi/12blanchi.html [accessed 13/2/2004].

CORES Registry website, www.cores-eu.net/registry/ [accessed 13/2/2004].

Day, M. (1999) *ROADS Interoperability Guidelines*, Bath, UKOLN, www.ukoln.ac.uk/metadata/roads/interoperability-guidelines/ [accessed 25/8/2003].

Dekkers, M., Causton, L., de Jong, A., Duval, E., Day, M. and Napier, M. (2001) *SCHEMAS Project. SCHEMAS-PwC-WP2-D28-Final-20011217* Metadata Watch Report 7, London, PricewaterhouseCoopers, www.schemas-forum.org/metadata-watch/d28/mwr7.htm [accessed 13/2/2004].

European Commission (2002) *DIFFUSE: Dissemination of InFormal and Formal Useful Specific Experiences to Research, Technology Development and Demonstration Communities*, IST-1999-13034, European Commission, Information Society Technologies Programme, www.ec-gis.org:8080/ wecgis/ECGIS.SYN_PROJECT.show?nome='535' [accessed 13/2/2004].

Hansen, J. and Andresen, L. (2003) *AC – Administrative Components. Dublin Core DCMI administrative metadata*, final version, http://dublincore.org/groups/admin/ [accessed 2/3/2004].

Hofman, P. and Worsfold, E. (1998) *Specification for Resource Description Methods Part 2: Selection Criteria for Quality Controlled Information Gateways*, Bristol, University of Bristol, www.ukoln.ac.uk/metadata/desire/quality/ [accessed 2/3/2004].

Holland, D. (2003) Creating a Metadata Application Profile for the MyOpen-Library Project, *Catalogue & Index*, **147**, Spring, 1–4.

Hunter, J. and Lagoze, C. (2001) Combining RDF and XML Schemas to Enhance Interoperability between Metadata Application Profiles. In *Proceedings of the 10th International World Wide Web Conference, held in Hong Kong, 1–5 May 2001*, www10.org/cdrom/papers/frame.html [accessed 13/2/2004].

Iannella, R. and Campbell, D. (1999) *The A-Core: metadata about content metadata, internet draft*, http://metadata.net/admin/draft-iannella-admin-01.txt [accessed 2/3/2004].

ISO 8601:2000. *Data Elements and Interchange Formats – Information Interchange – Representation of Dates and Times*, Geneva, International Organization for Standardization.

ISO 639-1:2002. *Codes for the Representation of Names of Languages – Part 1: Alpha-2-code*, Geneva, International Organization for Standardization.

Library of Congress (2003) METS: an overview and tutorial, Washington DC, Library of Congress, www.loc.gov/standards/mets/METSOverview. v2.html [accessed 13/2/2004].

McClelland, M., McArthur, D., Giersch, S and, Geisler, G. (2002) Challenges for Service Providers when Importing Metadata in Digital Libraries, DOI: 10.1045/april2002-mcclelland, *D-Lib Magazine*, **8** (4), www.dlib.org/dlib/april02/mcclelland/04mcclelland.html [accessed 13/2/2004].

Network Development and MARC Standards Office, Library of Congress (2001) *MARC to Dublin Core Crosswalk*, Library of Congress, www.loc.gov/marc/marc2dc.html [accessed 19/12/2003].

New Zealand e-Government Unit, State Services Commission (2001) *Metadata*

Management Facility User Requirements Specification, www.e-government.govt.nz/docs/mmf-users/mmf-users.pdf [accessed 13/2/2004].

SCHEMAS, www.schemas-forum.org/ [accessed 13/02/04].

Weibel, S. L. (1998) The Metadata Landscape: conventions for semantics, syntax and structure in the Internet Commons. In *Metadiversity. Proceedings of the Conference, held in Natural Bridge, VA, November 1998*, Philadelphia, PA, NFAIS, www.nfais.org/publications/metadiversity_preprints6.htm [accessed 13/2/2004].

Chapter 10
Looking forward – the future

overview

THIS CONCLUDING CHAPTER draws together the themes of this book and re-examines the five-point model of the purposes of metadata introduced in Chapter 1 and illustrated with examples in Chapters 4–8. Trends and possible future developments in metadata are described in terms of the model.

The chapter then looks at the durability of the metadata concept, how it will be perceived by the wider public and developments in the management of metadata. It speculates about the development of a coherent discipline or evolution of existing disciplines to incorporate metadata. The context is set for this by looking at the impact that metadata is having on related disciplines and research activity.

The chapter concludes with a statement of the conditions that will need to be met for the ongoing successful development of metadata as a means of managing and retrieving information.

Another look at the five-point model

The five-point model describes metadata in terms of its purposes. Although individual data elements may be used for more than one purpose, the purposes themselves remain distinct. So, for instance, there is a clear distinction between the title of a book as a description of that book and using words in the title for information retrieval. The model provides a way of examining metadata across a wide range of different application areas. A closer look at the model demonstrates why it works and provides some indication of how it might develop in the future.

Description and identification

Identification is seen as one aspect of description and is fundamental to other purposes. An identifier provides a 'handle' for a digital object and other information containers such as books, so that other processes such as retrieval, electronic trading or rights management can be performed.

The range of things being described using metadata will be extended in future. At present metadata is applied to works ranging from books to music and works of art. It is also applied to data collections and text-based electronic documents. There is some interest in developing metadata schemas to describe knowledge, especially tacit knowledge (the knowledge in people's heads). This suggests a view that people can be regarded as repositories for information. At the time of writing no major metadata standards have been developed for knowledge management, although some proprietary systems may have data dictionary definitions that could form the basis for a future metadata schemes for knowledge.

As discussed earlier, a key to description is the ability to identify what is being described by the metadata. There are a number of standalone identifier standards that can be incorporated into metadata schemes such as ISBNs for books, GRids in the music industry, and DOIs for text. In some industries there are competing or overlapping identifier systems and it would be reasonable to anticipate some consolidation in this area with the emergence of a single, universal identifier system for all kinds of entity. The problem is to determine at what level the identifier should be applied. For instance a work can have its own identifier, so can individual editions of a book, each with its own ISBN, and so can individual items in a collection – typically identified by an accession number, a barcode or an RFID (radio-frequency identifier) chip.

Retrieval

The second purpose of metadata is one that has attracted more commentary and speculation than any other. It is the focus of a great deal of the work on metadata standards for web resources, such as Dublin Core. The retrieval purpose ties in the description as a means of evaluating a resource when it has been retrieved.

Retrieval is developing on a number of fronts, image retrieval being one of the most interesting areas at the moment. Image retrieval presents particular challenges of interpretation. For example, what is the most significant element of a picture? What does it mean? Automated image indexing depends on shape, colour and texture, but does not address the 'meaning' or interpretation of an image. Some images have very clearly defined attributes. A language for the description of images will evolve so that a standard vocabulary can be used to index images. This will improve searching across and retrieval from several collections at once.

Indexing is one of the ways of improving retrieval performance. However, the costs of indexing are high and there are continued efforts to find ways of automating this process. The development of heuristic systems to analyse and categorize text-based works is already well advanced, but they depend on human intervention to set up classification systems or subject terminologies that reflect the areas being indexed. Some heuristic systems do not use controlled vocabulary, but work on the basis of feedback from users to build up a 'picture' of what the user wants. The heuristic systems are based on experience and not necessarily codified into any formal rules. One outcome of this development may be less dependence on formally applied indexing and less emphasis on the use of metadata specifically earmarked for retrieval. When dealing with digital objects, systems will search the text in the object itself and analyse it directly, rather than depending on human-generated analyses found in keywords and classification terms.

Management of resources

Management of information has become a very large and diverse area, ranging from records management to preservation of electronic publications and library management systems. These areas can be drawn together by the lifecycle concept. The management of information can be viewed in terms of managing the lifecycle of an information resource, using metadata to achieve this.

One of the key challenges is to manage information effectively and consistently. Metadata standards help this process by making the job of application developers easier. Metadata provides a conceptualization of the entities that need to be handled by an application. As application areas mature, accepted practice will be codified in metadata standards which can then be applied across a market. This can be seen in the records management field where metadata standards have been a key feature of the specifications for Electronic Document and Records Management (EDRM) systems. The specifications have in effect defined the market for these products and have also created a pool of products that (in theory at least) allows clients to migrate their data from one product to another. In future, this approach to defining the market through metadata standards might be expected to operate in other sectors. Common metadata standards make it easier to upgrade and transfer data from one system to another. One of the challenges will be to ensure that there is sufficient compatibility in the encoding systems used to allow true comparability of data and to lay the foundations for interoperability and e-commerce.

Rights and provenance

Rights and ownership are very closely tied in to one another and it is difficult to separate the purposes. Establishing the ownership of information is a pre-requisite of managing the commercial and intellectual property rights. Provenance is connected to the ownership of an information resource, although not necessarily with the intellectual property rights. There is a great deal of overlap between ownership and provenance. A description of provenance depends on the lifecycle of an information resource. Ownership of the resource and the management processes that have taken place need to be auditable, in order to establish its provenance.

Rights management is very topical, particularly in the context of music and video recording. The technology for recording digital materials is now so inexpensive that piracy has become a major issue for the recording industry. Downloading of music via the internet, even when legitimate, raises problems of paying fees and royalties based on use of individual items.

Making a rights management system cost-effective and practical from the point of view of rights owners and retailers, systems will require the consolidation of transactional data in different ways, for instance:

- by customer – for charging
- by rights owner – for payment of royalties
- by outlet – for management.

One development will be the move towards more micro-transactions based on the purchase of individual items rather than collections of items. In the music industry this might be individual music tracks from an album; in the publishing industry it might be individual articles from a journal issue. This can be done by attaching metadata to the tradeable items (particularly if this is done via the internet), which may be an ID such as a Digital Object Identifier, or may contain additional metadata such as the name of the rights owner, the conditions of use and the item price. E-commerce systems record the transactions so that consolidations can be made and the customers billed accordingly. It also means that the appropriate royalties are paid to the correct person when they are due.

Verifying the authenticity of data is another area of growing concern. Many organizations are moving away from archiving paper records to digital preservation and management of electronic records. Providing an audit trail of individual documents will become increasingly important to validate their content and to 'prove' their authenticity and integrity. Electronic documents are perceived as being susceptible to alteration after they have been finalized. In practice changes to paper and electronic documents are both detectable, although different approaches may be needed to identify changes. Metadata embedded in electronic documents can provide evidence of tampering. Many common office applications generate their own metadata which includes a trail of alterations made to the document throughout its life. An obvious step would be to standardize this type of metadata. The International Organization for Standardization has already produced guidelines on the legal admissibility of electronic documents (ISO 12654:1997). Some legislatures have responded by allowing properly maintained and documented electronic records to be treated as primary sources of information or evidence. Others will move in this direction.

Interoperability

Metadata is an enabler of interoperability. Metadata provides a way of describing the data handled by different systems and gives a focus for compatibility of data passed between systems. This is a prerequisite for e-commerce systems, which are based on the interoperation of different systems at different stages in the supply chain.

This is probably most advanced in the book industry, which has developed standards for describing publications and for handling transactions related to the trade of publications. This approach will be extended to other sectors as electronic trading becomes more widespread and more consumer-oriented. This will mean smaller individual transactions and greater confidence in the authentication procedures.

Interoperability also plays a key role in the effective delivery of library services to users. Common metadata standards allow for the exchange of data between institutions and for the transfer of metadata records (catalogue records) from one system to another. This is essential for the operation of union catalogues where a user can search the holdings of several libraries simultaneously.

Developments in e-government and, in particular, electronic service delivery will also depend on interoperability of systems to provide a coherent, consistent and integrated approach to the customer or citizen. In order for this to happen some work will be needed to consolidate existing metadata standards.

Development of the model

The five-point model of the purposes of metadata is a useful device to help thinking about the current state of metadata. It addresses some of the shortcomings of previous models, and like them provides a means to understanding metadata at one point in time. It stands up to scrutiny in the context of metadata in the library and information field as it is now. However, it may need to evolve to reflect the future development of metadata.

Trends in metadata management

Standards development

The standards development process is often prompted by the proliferation of incompatible systems in response to a practical problem. As accepted good practices emerge, standards are often developed to codify that practice and provide a common approach. This is fundamental to the successful operation of metadata systems.

One of the most widely used metadata schemes, the Dublin Core Metadata Element Set, is now an international standard (ISO 15836:2003). It provides a starting point for many application profiles developed by specific communities and individual organizations. We have seen for instance how it has been extended by the UK's Office of the e-Envoy to create the e-GMS standard (UK Office of the e-Envoy, 2003).

Standards development is a helpful way of negotiating a system that all parties can work with. This is evident in the publishing industry and book trade which is made up of conflicting and competing interests and yet co-operated to develop the ONIX metadata system, because of the need of the different parties to exchange data. Another example is the evolution of the national MARC standards into MARC21, a unified international standard (Library of Congress, 2003). ISO 2709:1996 (equivalent to

NISO/ANSI Z39.2) defines the format that MARC needs to be encoded in for exchange.

Information models

The move towards common models for analysing metadata elements and the relationships between them will continue. Schemas such as the Resource Discovery Framework lend themselves to expression using XML as a mark-up language. Assuming the continued importance of the internet and its protocols for internal and external communications, XML-enabled schemas for metadata are likely to become the norm.

This book has presented a range of modelling systems such as OAI, RDF and FRBR and the overlap between them has been discussed. There may be some consolidation of these models in future or development of new models that incorporate features from these existing systems to allow greater interoperability. There will also be closer links between the way in which data modelling systems are used to analyse information resources and the creation of metadata standards. An example of this is the way in which FRBR is being used to inform the development of the revised AACR rules and the potential impact this will have on the MARC21 standard.

Is metadata here to stay?

A review of the five-point model of metadata raises a more fundamental question: is metadata here to stay? There is always a suspicion that a new concept or way of thinking is merely a fad that will pass very quickly. An alternative view is that a new concept can become an accepted part of the normal operation of systems to the degree that it is barely recognized as a separate activity – it becomes a part of a wider discipline.

Metadata has been around a long time: for at least 2500 years in the form of library catalogues. During that time it has been transformed into something with a wide range of applications and operating at very sophisticated levels of detail. It will continue to exist and evolve and a community of specialists will continue to work on the development of data models and metadata standards. It also plays a fundamental part in e-commerce systems and this type of application area will continue to develop.

The balance of the purposes may change. For example, retrieval systems may become more dependent on artificial intelligence systems that are able to analyse the text of information resources and to generate effective retrieval strategies in response to user queries. It is possible that these approaches might replace metadata that is currently used for retrieval, such as subject keywords or classification codes assigned by indexers.

What changes?

Invisible future

Metadata is becoming more ubiquitous as it is incorporated into a wide range of systems and applications. The incorporation of metadata schemas into application profiles is already helping the development of new products and services on the market. These systems have metadata definitions and handling capabilities built into them. Some of the metadata is visible to users, but a lot of it is invisible to users and intended for exchange of data between different applications during transactions. Metadata use is potentially an area of growth with the drive to greater interoperability between systems. Interoperability will allow different applications such as word-processors and spreadsheet packages to attach metadata to documents, which can be picked up by EDRM systems. The development of systems-oriented metadata will continue to grow rapidly and it is possible that users may become less aware of metadata. A community of specialists will be needed to develop the metadata standards and implement the resulting schemas. However, the metadata will be seen as a tool for making systems and applications work effectively.

Education and research

Although the general user will be less aware of metadata, certain communities will have more to do with it. There was considerable growth in the activity surrounding metadata in the late 1990s and before that activity devoted to certain communities such as the geospatial and statistical communities. Awareness of metadata has only recently become more widespread among information professionals and the IT community. This awareness is beginning to have an impact on systems developers, who are now thinking specifically in terms of metadata as a way of managing data, controlling its format and building in interoperability.

The more dynamic parts of the information disciplines are changing to incorporate metadata as a part of their range of knowledge and skills. An increasing number of library and information science academic courses now include metadata as a part of the syllabus. This trend will continue and in time a new interdisciplinary subject may emerge. Already bodies such as the European Commission have provided research funding to investigate metadata further. The recognition of metadata as a discipline in its own right could help to facilitate the convergence of practice and interests among the sectors that make extensive use of it. Several different metadata traditions have developed and a lot of activity is currently focused on reconciling the different approaches and to finding new metadata models and standards that reflect the best of current practice and allow for greater inter-operation of metadata standards.

One possible result of this closer working together will be the development of common models for metadata and this could form the basis of a new subject or discipline. It could also form the basis of future research activity in the academic community.

summary

The role of metadata today and in the future can be summarized by the following points:

- Metadata has five distinct purposes.
- It is here to stay.
- Metadata will be an integral part of information systems.
- Metadata will be invisible to most users.
- Metadata development will progress through co-operation between communities of interest.
- There is a need for a universal model for metadata to encourage further development of this subject.

References and further sources of information

Buchanan, M. (2001) *Ubiquity: the science of history, or why the world is simpler than we think*, Weidenfeld and Nicolson, 2000.

FRBR, www.ifla.org/VII/s13/wgfrbr/wgfrbr.htm [accessed 15/2/2004].

ISO 2709:1996. *Information and Documentation – Format for Information Exchange*, Geneva, International Organization for Standardization.

ISO 12654:1997. *Electronic Imaging – Recommendations for the management of electronic recording systems for the recording of documents that may be required as evidence, on WORM systems for the recording of documents that may be required as evidence, on WORM optical disk*, Geneva, International Organization for Standardization.

ISO 15836:2003. *Information and Documentation – The Dublin Core Metadata Element Set*, Geneva, International Organization for Standardization.

Library of Congress (2003) *MARC 21. Concise format for bibliographic data*, concise edn, Washington DC, Library of Congress, http://lcweb.loc.gov/marc/bibliographic [accessed 5/2/2004].

UK Office of the e-Envoy (2003) *E-Government Metadata Standard with XML Syntax*, Version 2.0, London, Cabinet Office.

Index

RMD *see* DOI Record Metadata Declaration
robots 87
RoMEO project 124

schemas 25–27, 108
    selecting 150–1, 162
SCHEMAS project 150, 161
Scottish Cultural Resources Access Network *see* SCRAN
SCRAN 60–1
search aids 165–6
search engines 85–7
searching 93–4
security 164–5
    records classification 103
security systems 72
semantic interoperability 138, 159
semantic web 94
serials 71
SGML 22
Shannon's Information Theory 84
Simple Object Access Protocol *see* SOAP
SOAP 32
spiders 87
Standard Generalized Mark-up Language *see* SGML
standards 50–61, 175–6
    de facto 50–1
    e-GMS 56
    electronic rights trading 131
    government information 55–6
    industry 50–1
    international 50–1
    national 50–1
    proprietary 50–1
statements, *see* RDF statements
stock control 72
structural interoperability 160
subject indexing *see* indexing
surrogacy 109
synonyms 85, 88
syntactic interoperability 160

tagging 24
taxonomies 89–91, 153–4
    records management 105
territorial rights 122
text retrieval 80–2
textual analysis 98, 155
thesauri 88, 89–91, 153
Title element 73–4
tracking 72
training of users *see* user education
transliteration 75

UKOnline 86
uniform resource locators *see* URLs
Uniform Resource Names *see* URNs
union catalogues 32
URLs 68, 70
URNs 68
user education 166

verification 165
versioning 107–9
V-ISAN 72

web community 51–2
web content *see* content management
web gateways 91–3
web portals 91–3
word processing 30
work *see* FRBR Work
workflow 107–9
works, text works 71

XML 23
XML schemas *see* schemas
XSDL 25

Z39.50 32
Z39.50 International Next Generation *see* ZING
ZING 32